WHERE THE OLD
ROSES GROW

WHERE THE OLD ROSES GROW

Vita Sackville-West and the Battle
for Beauty during Wartime

Janelle McCulloch

Published in 2024
A Pimpernel Press book for Gemini Adult Books Ltd
part of the Gemini Books Group

Based in Woodbridge and London

Marine House, Tide Mill Way,
Woodbridge, Suffolk, IP12 1AP
United Kingdom

www.geminibooks.com

Text © 2024 Janelle McCulloch

ISBN 978-1-914902-18-5

A CIP catalogue record for this book is
available from the British Library.

Every reasonable effort has been made to trace copyright-holders of
material reproduced in this book, but if any have been inadvertently
overlooked the publishers would be glad to hear from them.

Design and typeset by Danny Lyle

Printed in the UK
10 9 8 7 6 5 4 3 2 1

I would like to dedicate this book to Vita Sackville-West, Constance Spry, Maud Messel, Graham Stuart Thomas and Edward Bunyard — five fine rosarians who changed the course of horticultural history with their passion for old roses.

I would also like to dedicate this book to the wonderful rosarians, gardeners, garden designers and writers I met during my research. These include but are not limited to Adam Nicolson, Troy Scott Smith, Isabel and Julian Bannerman, Victoria Martin of Stokesay Walled Garden, and Charles and Brigid Quest-Ritson. All of the people and sources consulted are included in the complete bibliography at the end of this book, along with a list of all those who kindly granted me an interview.

CONTENTS

A Note about Old Roses

Roses can loosely be divided into old and modern. Old roses – sometimes referred to as heritage, historic, antique or old-fashioned roses – are those bred from the late eighteenth century to the early nineteenth century. They include species (the original wild roses), Gallicas, Damasks, Albas, Centifolias, Moss roses, Bourbons, Hybrid Perpetuals, China roses, Teas, Noisettes and Ramblers. The modern roses, such as Hybrid Teas, Floribundas, Grandifloras, Miniatures and Climbers, were developed later and are more like bedding roses, with a short, upright habit (although shrub roses have a more informal habit and may sometimes be quite tall and arching). Two of the defining characteristics of old roses are their shape and their scent. The flowers are often extravagant in form, usually with multiple petals and layers, and their fragrance is almost always remarkable. They are plants of beauty, glamour, grandeur and grace.

'Small pleasures must correct great tragedies.'
Vita Sackville-West, *The Garden*

1

The Writer
and the Ruin

'Our gardens assert a powerful hold on our
collective imaginations; they are reflections of our secret
selves, places of memory and nostalgia in which we
perform complex rituals of hope and stewardship.'

Alex Preston,
writing about author Penelope Lively in *The Guardian*,
October 2017

The spring of 1930 was a season of great anxiety in southern England. But it was also a season of gentle pleasures. The Great Depression, which had started with a stock market crash in New York in October 1929 and then floated to England on a dark cloud of winter misery, had hit many British businesses. But when spring arrived in 1930, with its promise of milder temperatures and calmer, daffodil-filled days, people felt a tinge of optimism in their weary hearts. Many Londoners chose to celebrate the spring season, as they do every year, with picnics and walks in parks, or outings to the cinema or the countryside (the railways put on organised hikes). In London's Covent Garden Market, the famous flower-sellers welcomed spring's new blooms by trading cut flowers as fast as their muscled arms could carry them. By April 1930, there were more than 2,000 'basket men' carrying wicker baskets of flowers around Covent Garden, many using their heads to balance the woven towers. Cecil Beaton was just one of the customers who visited the market each Friday, taking his bouquets to the country to dress his rooms in tulips and other blooms. These joyful excursions served as a distraction from London's distressed economy, and from the Nazi party across the Channel, which was growing in noise and numbers. People were yearning for beauty after the prolonged misery of winter. They were waiting, as they did every year, for the great floraison.

In Kent, in south-east England, spring was slow to arrive. It would come, but not before a series of deluges. For the first few days of April, storm clouds scudded across the Weald, until finally they broke to bespatter the hills and fields in downpours. Umbrellas opened in the county's villages like giant mushrooms sprouting from the streets.

Friday, 4 April was a particularly bitter day, with an irascible wind that refused to go away. At her home at Long Barn, the writer Victoria

('Vita') Sackville-West dressed warmly for an outing – an inspection of a castle in the small hamlet of Sissinghurst, near Cranbrook. Vita normally adored April: it was the season when, as she later penned in her book *Country Notes in Wartime*, 'cherry, plum, pear and thorn whiten the orchards.' But on this spring morning there were few white petals to be seen. Nevertheless, she was animated with anticipation. With her was her younger son, thirteen-year-old Nigel Nicolson, and her friend and former lover, Dorothy 'Dottie' Wellesley, later Duchess of Wellington. It was Dottie who had heard about Sissinghurst from a land agent she knew, a Mr Beale. 'It is a Victorian farmhouse,' Dottie told Vita, with 'picturesque ruins in the grounds'. Mr Beale had admitted to Dottie that it had languished on the market for two years. Not surprisingly, nobody wanted to buy a ruin. Not in 1930.

Vita's spring excursion to look at properties could not have come at a better time in her life. For the past decade, she and her husband, Harold Nicolson, and their two sons had been living at Long Barn, a fourteenth-century house that the couple had bought in 1915. It was the place where they had made their first garden together. It seemed idyllic from the outside, but Vita and Harold's marriage was far from perfect. Although they were loving towards each other, the couple had struggled with various issues for some time. Harold was a diplomat, soon to be a Member of Parliament, and was, according to his granddaughter Juliet Nicolson, 'clever, funny, vital, and an effervescent person'. Vita, in contrast, was incredibly shy, though gifted with wit and striking facial features. In a photo taken at this time, her thick dark hair frames a face of intelligence and grace; a face that, while not quite conventionally beautiful, is of someone you would like to sit next to at a dinner party. Vita loved Harold, but she also admired clever, beautiful women, who often fell for her charisma in return. Her affairs, however – especially her liaison with author and socialite Violet Trefusis – had upended her marriage at times. And then when Harold and Vita learned that the farm next to Long Barn was being sold to a battery chicken farmer, they must have felt desperate for a change, both in their marital life and in their home.

Unfortunately, the weather on Friday, 4 April was in no mood to frame a prospective estate. The rain from a wet March month had softened all the paths to mud. When the expectant group arrived, they were forced to step around the puddles. For Dottie, the squalid buildings were a shock. She probably expected more of a *cottage orné*. Vita's son Nigel was similarly horrified, particularly by the prospect of *living* there. Vita, however, was undiscouraged. With her characteristic energy, she enthusiastically explored the gathering of neglected buildings, including the Elizabethan tower. Only the Tudor entrance was inhabited – by farm labourers and horses. The rest of it was a derelict mess of farm rubbish, punctuated with bedsteads, old toilets, rustic balls of entwined farm wire, farm ploughs, and – inexplicably – mountains of sardine tins. Two decades later, in 1950, Vita recalled her first impressions for *House & Garden* magazine: 'There was nothing but a dreadful mess of old chicken houses and wire chicken runs; broken-down spile fences; rubbish dumps where cottagers had piled their tins, their bottles, their rusty ironmongery and their broken crockery for perhaps half a century; old cabbage stalks; and a tangle of weeds everywhere. Brambles grew in wild profusion; bindweed wreathed its way into every support; ground-elder made a green carpet; docks and nettles flourished; couch-grass sprouted.'

There was no electricity at Sissinghurst. No water. There was not a single, decent, ready-to-move-in room. The only habitable dwelling was the nearby Castle Farmhouse. But Vita did not want the farmhouse. She wanted the ruined castle.

Sissinghurst had some merits. The ancient brick walls were pretty, Vita noted, and they gave the garden the feel of a *hortus conclusus*. But the rest of the place was a forlorn scene.

Undaunted, Vita looked up at the tower, which rose above it all. She imagined it as a writer's retreat, surrounded by rose gardens. She surveyed the long, misty views over the gentle Kent landscape, and then walked through the run-down kitchen garden, the orchard of old apple trees, and the remnants of a nuttery. She could see how it could all be transformed from ruin to botanic reverie. How, in summer, the warmth would reflect off the ancient bricks, the climbing roses would clothe and embroider the buildings and gather on the tops of windows and doors to meet in scented narrative, and the flower beds would be filled with nodding perennials. Most of all, she could see that Sissinghurst would be perfect for growing her favourite flower: the old-fashioned rose. 'The old walls were the perfect backdrop for the [roses'] untidy, lavish habit [and] here was space a-plenty, with the walls to frame their exuberance,' she later recalled. Standing in the middle of an old cabbage patch, she turned to Nigel and said: 'I think we shall be happy in this place.'

Ninety-three years after that seminal day in April 1930, I made my own journey to Sissinghurst on a warm summer's evening in June 2023. It was not my first visit – I used to live in London, and Sissinghurst has always been my favourite garden. But this was a special occasion. I was joining a small group for a light dinner in Sissinghurst's garden after the public had left for the day, for a kind of casual, intimate *fête champêtre*.

The summer sky that night was beguiling – the almost irides-cent blue of a kingfisher's plumage. As our small group drank their champagne and ate their canapés, I left them and quietly entered the walled rose garden, where the roses were at that perfect stage when they expand from bud to full bloom. There were no visitors in the garden, no gardeners pruning, no noise but the sound of the breeze through the trees and the distant hum of our little group chatting beneath Vita's tower. It felt as though I had slipped back in time. I half-expected Vita to walk through the brick arch, secateurs in hand.

An hour or so later, as the pink twilight settled on the Kent land-scape, we each took a seat around the steps of the tower to listen to a talk by Vita's grandson, Adam Nicolson, and her granddaughter Juliet about growing up here, in this pastoral idyll. For one night the garden had become a *salon de verdure*.

Adam began by giving the family's account of what happened on that germinal afternoon in the spring of 1930.

'The brokenness that Vita felt, after Knole had been sold and Long Barn was about to be hemmed by battery chicken farms, meant that she needed to find somewhere of her own,' he said, with his grandmother's gift for storytelling. 'So, on a dreadfully rainy day in 1930, she came across Sissinghurst.' He paused, and I am certain that our little group leaned forward. 'We still have the ad for Sissinghurst. It read: "Farmhouse for sale." And then, on page eleven, the advert finally mentioned: "Ruins in grounds".' I had heard this account many times, but never the 'page eleven' version. 'My granny Vita came with her then-girlfriend Dottie and brought my father. They inspected this broken-down hideous mess of a place. And after a while Vita said: "I think we will be very happy here". My father said it was the worst day of his life!'

Then Juliet Nicolson stepped in. Sissinghurst, she said, was 'a mesmerically beautiful place'. It was, she felt, 'meant to be'. Ruin and writer. Destined to meet.

'The centuries had wrecked it, and by 1930 it was little more than a few brick fragments sitting among sheep fields and creaking apple trees. It was exactly that state of ruination, pleading for redemption, that appealed to my grandmother,' Adam once wrote in an editorial for the *New York Times*, and he reiterated this point on this calm summer evening. Sissinghurst, he summarised eloquently, was 'an act of theatre'. It was a home and garden made by 'a poet with romance in her heart'.

Vita was not the first to be seduced by a ruin and she will not be the last. Many gardeners dream of finding a lost or secret garden, perhaps because such idylls come with what the celebrated garden designer Isabel Bannerman calls a 'illusory, hallucinatory quality'. In Sissinghurst Vita seemed to find a place where time had stopped, a place where she could catch her breath. It is almost as if she knew Sissinghurst would be beneficial for her; for her nerves and her mind, and probably her writing as well.

As many biographers have noted, Sissinghurst looked a little like Knole, Vita's beloved childhood home. Both have what is essentially a mediaeval design of a smaller walled garden inside an outer one. Sissinghurst even featured a main arched gatehouse set into a long building, and similar arched windows at the front, as Knole does. I interviewed Sissinghurst's Cultural Heritage Curator, Rowena Willard-Wright for this biography, and she agreed. Vita, said Rowena, would have recognised the similarities to Knole right away. Vita would also have noted that the garden was private, protected from the world. 'Sissinghurst has always had the feeling of being enclosed, safe, secure,' agreed Rowena. 'It has these great walls, and walls within walls, such as Vita's tower. It would have offered the perfect retreat for her.'

Whatever fired Vita's imagination on that grey April day, her mind was made up. She was going to buy it, ruin and all. When she returned home that afternoon to tell her husband what she had found, Harold Nicolson, like a true diplomat, kept his thoughts in check.

The next day, Saturday 5 April 1930, was equally as sodden. Vita, Harold and their other son Benedict (Ben) decided to return to Sissinghurst for another inspection. Vita drove there with their dogs, winding her way through the soaked countryside. Ben and Harold, who probably preferred neatness and order over dog saliva and damp car seats, caught the train to Staplehurst, where Vita met them at the station. Harold was dressed in his usual dapper fashion: a well-fitted jacket with a pocket handkerchief, and tailored trousers the same rich, compost-brown colour and texture as his moustache. Vita and Harold were both familiar with the Kent countryside, and knew what to expect, of fashion and of field. Vita knew the ancient undulating hills of the Kentish Weald as well as the folds in her own woollen skirts. She was quietly optimistic of the prospect of finding a new home in this part of England that she and Harold both loved.

As the last of the rainstorms cleared and a sliver of blue tried to break through, she must have felt a glimmer of anticipation, as though spring had finally arrived, and they were about to experience something special. Blinking through the low-slanting spring light, the family pulled up in the courtyard and walked around the estate. Vita pointed out the fine brick walls remaining from the Elizabethan period, perhaps suggesting to Harold that they offered the perfect backdrop for a walled garden – one filled with romantic antique roses: Gallicas, Albas, Damasks, Mosses – heritage roses for an architectural folly, lost to time. Finally, at the end of their tour, they turned a corner and there before them was a sad tangle of a rare Gallica rose – a 'shrubby woody old rose', as Vita later noted. The rose had clearly been holding on for years: a gentle ghost of the garden's former glory.

After Adam Nicolson finished his talk on the steps of Vita's tower, embellished with stories from his sister Juliet, he kindly offered to show me the location of the rose that Vita had discovered on that wet spring afternoon in 1930. He sprinted off through the White Garden, and I tried to follow. He has a long stride and the hedged English box path in the White Garden is narrow, so I tried to keep pace, gently pushing away the perennials that fell over the hedged borders. Summer had arrived late that year, after a long, cool spring in England, so the White Garden was a curious mix of flowers that should have gone over weeks ago and those that were just opening: waving spring irises, jolly lupins and towering foxgloves. We headed for the giant yew hedges and emerged on the other side into the orchard and the wildflower meadow around it. I was immediately struck by the stillness. There were few people around. The evening light was gilded as the sun set behind Vita's tower. I felt, not the first time, that we had slipped back in time.

Adam pointed to a quiet place in the corner of the wildflower meadow, beside the moat. 'This is where Vita found the rose when she first saw Sissinghurst,' he says. 'It was a Gallica, an old rose. A lovely cerise-coloured rose. In 1930, there was no garden, of course, and this orchard was full of rubbish and debris. Sissinghurst had been empty for two years, the historic Elizabethan house had gone. There is an old saying with Elizabethan gardens: you should look down at a garden from the north. So this must have once been a beautiful garden, right here, where this rose was. This is all that survived, this rose. The whole place had disintegrated, and yet the rose had survived.'

I was entranced. Did Vita see it as a sign? 'No.' Adam was pragmatic. 'I don't think she felt that. I think she was just astounded.'

Vita later wrote about this rose in 1950 (*House & Garden*). 'The only thing we found of any interest was an old *Gallica* rose, then unknown to cultivation, which is now listed as *Gallica* var. 'Sissinghurst Castle'. Miss Nancy Lindsay, who is an expert on such matters, says that my old rose is *Gallica* 'Tour des Maures', a great rarity.'

The rose, with a beautiful plum-coloured flower described by David Austin as 'particularly tough', is said to date from before 1850. It is now called, simply, 'Sissinghurst Castle'. Adam added that the rose was moved to the end of the orchard. He then excused himself to say goodbye to the rest of the guests, and I thanked him for his company, and walked further along the moat, in the direction of the summer house, to find it. There, I found a rose that may or may not have been the famous 'Sissinghurst Castle' rose. But it mattered little, because I found something just as memorable: a view of Vita's tower that I had never seen, as it shimmered in the evening light. I wondered what Vita thought, on that miserable day in April 1930, when she decided to throw caution to the Kent wind and buy an abandoned castle? Did she stand in this very spot, looking back at the ancient tower, framed by the setting sun? Was she at all daunted by the prospect of buying this derelict estate? She must have had an enormous faith in herself – and in Harold – when she signed the contract. (Although Vita and Harold considered Sissinghurst their joint property, Vita bought it with her money.) Or was she entranced by the idea of restoring this great estate, saving it from ruin? And, perhaps, in doing so, saving herself. As the biographer and writer Matthew Dennison wrote of Vita in the brilliant biography *Behind the Mask*: 'She had a poet-gardener's belief in the redemptive power of beauty.'

There is a saying in publishing: stories find their authors. Perhaps the same can be said of gardens. Perhaps gardens find their custodians at a time when they need those custodians most. Who knows if it is true, but Vita was determined to buy Sissinghurst. And, in her, it seemed to have found the perfect guardian. (Later, Vita realised it had once been occupied by some of her ancestors, in the 1530s.) But Sissinghurst would also be Vita's saviour in many ways. The tower would help her to write, while the garden would give her peace, even during her most troubled years. Sissinghurst and its tower and garden would be the one constant in Vita's life, even when she was distracted by her books, her lovers, her travels, her marriage, and the greatest disruption of all – war.

Harold, always the pragmatist, tried to reason with Vita. But she was not to be dissuaded. Finally, he relented. On 7 May 1930, the couple bought it. A good thing it was, too. 'Vita', wrote Harold in his diary, 'had already fallen flat in love.'

The next day, as the summer heat started to increase and London's streets began to warm from the ground up, I walked from my hotel, The Lime Tree in Belgravia (a bolthole loved by gardeners), to the John Sandoe bookshop on the King's Road. The bookshop, a favourite with lovers of design and garden books, seems to be held together by creaky stairs and old bookshelves full of books, and on this day was heavy with temperature and atmosphere in equal measure. I was there to buy Adam Nicolson's latest book, *How to Be: Lessons from the Early Greeks*. Afterwards, I walked along the King's Road to Waterstones, where they had air conditioning and a copy of my book, *Gardens of Style*, which I bought to give to Adam as a gift. The young girl at Waterstones' counter, Zuleika, saw the cover of my book and commented on it. I confessed that it was my own book and that I was giving it to the grandson of Vita Sackville-West. 'Oh!' she exclaimed. 'I have just finished reading Vita's novel *All Passions Spent*. I finished it yesterday. I borrowed it from the library and loved it so much I went out and bought two copies for my parents to read. I love Vita's writing! I did not know much about her, but I am determined to find more of her books.' I was delighted for her and then I asked her how old she was, because I thought: *This would be a lovely side story to include in the biography.* 'Twenty-three,' she said. Twenty-three ... I asked Zuleika if she had a garden of her own. 'A tiny balcony one, but I am learning fast,' she said. 'Vita is teaching me.' I took down her email and we promised to stay in touch. I suspected that Vita would have been delighted with her joyful enthusiasm.

As I walked back to the hotel, I remembered how, a year before, I had made another journey to Sissinghurst to look through Vita's family photo albums. It had been a sun-filled autumn day in October. I had left my hotel located near Kew Gardens at 5.55 a.m. and taken two long train rides to arrive at Staplehurst station a few hours later. A kindly taxi driver drove me through the country roads to Sissinghurst village and then down the winding lane to the castle itself. The garden had not yet opened, so I walked down to the end of the moat, through a turnstile, past a walker with a jolly black spaniel doing loops and leaps and bounds, and through a field full of grazing sheep before turning and walking back again. The only sound in the still of the autumn morning was the clip-clip-clip of the gardeners pruning some of the famous roses on the external walls. The garden had reached its autumn fecundity. It was wild and ebullient and wonderfully abundant. I thought of Vita, striding these paths where I was walking now. And I thought of Julian Bannerman's fabulous line in the Nowness video about Trematon Castle, *Great*

Gardens: Trematon Castle: 'A lot of people don't see gardens early in the morning. And I always think it is a sad thing. I mean all the great gardens like Sissinghurst – people lived in them, got drunk in them, argued in them, saw dawns and dusks in them. We all see them very sanitised now.' I looked through the orchard, trying to imagine Vita discussing with Harold where to plant things, making garden notes and future plans.

At the bookshop, Sissinghurst's Cultural Heritage Curator Rowena Willard-Wright introduced herself, and together we made our way through the old servants' quarters and then a maze of upstairs spaces to a tiny archival room at the end, overlooking Vita's famous Purple Border, where intensely coloured dahlias were nodding hello to the first of the day's visitors. There were surprisingly few boxes, books or archives to look through. I wondered whether Rowena was too busy to find much for me, or perhaps weary of people wanting to go through these files. I was not perturbed. I was just grateful to see Vita's private photos. I was looking for any nuances of Vita's life that I may have missed in the years of research.

The biggest problem I faced was that Vita's life had been discussed so much, in both biographies and media articles over the years, that it had almost been over-analysed. Was there anything left to uncover?

Here, on this golden autumn morning, looking at her private photos from 1930, I began to feel that there was. In her famous breeches, her floral Liberty-style shirt and her enormous gardening hat, she seemed both modern and glamorous, but also enigmatic. Her expression was unreadable, even for a journalist like me who has interviewed hundreds of people, from prime ministers to drunken rock stars, and read unreadable expressions.

I was intrigued.

An hour later, I met Sissinghurst's head gardener Troy Scott Smith, who has been gardening at Sissinghurst, on and off, for thirty years – almost as long as Vita. I asked him what he thought Vita was like. Even though he had never met her, I suspected he had a feel for her by now, after reading her notes and writings every week. He paused before answering, and finally replied: 'She was very observant.' *Observant.* It was the same word Sarah Raven, Vita's granddaughter-in-law (who is married to Adam Nicolson), used in an interview with *Harper's Bazaar* in

March 2014, in the lead-up to the publication of Sarah's own biography. *Observant.* What did Troy and Sarah mean? Half an hour later, after I had finished my interview with Troy and returned to the archive room, I looked at the photo of Vita again, where she was looking directly back at the camera. I could see what Troy meant. Vita had the perceptive, steady gaze of a writer who notices everything around them. But more than that, she had a gardener's eye. She was somebody who observed the world, and all its intricacies, nuances, landscapes, light and layers. Day after day. Season after season. Year after year.

(Side note: during the research into this biography, I found a recording of Vita's voice on YouTube, of all places. She is reading passages from her poem *The Land*, recorded by Columbia in 1931, the year after she bought Sissinghurst. She is 39 but has the vocal control of a BBC broadcaster with fifty years of experience. As someone wrote in the comments below the recording, it is rare to hear this diction; the closest anyone has probably come is the editor and author Diana Athill. Vita's voice is clipped in places where we now expand, and expanded in places where would now clip. She pronounces poem, for example, as po-em, drawing the vowel 'o' out so long you are caught up in the romance of the word as you wait for the pronunciation to end. *Po-em.* It is the melodious voice of a poet.)

The other thing that was apparent to me from Vita's photos in her private albums was just how derelict Sissinghurst was in 1930. There is no polite way to frame it: Sissinghurst was, as Vita's son Nigel, put it when he first saw it, a *dump.* Vita and Harold's photos clearly showed the overgrowth, the years of debris, the agricultural detritus. There were even cumulations of old toilets. One photo, which Vita had captioned June 1930, showed a white picket fence valiantly trying to stand upright amidst a sea of encroaching brambles and bushes. Next to it is Vita's tower, but there is also an ancient greenhouse in the photo (I learned later that it was dismantled long ago), which was being overtaken by tangled mounds of ivy, nettles, hawthorn and other weeds.

I looked out of the ancient windows, comparing the scene I was seeing in present-day Sissinghurst to the one in the black-and-white photos beneath my hands. So much had changed in the garden, but the two constants between 1930 and 2022 were the architecture and the light. The light on this October morning was changing from the silver of the post-dawn hours to the warm bronze of an autumn day, and as the garden began to fill with visitors, wearing jaunty hats and natty raincoats slung over their arms, I could see why Vita was won over.

'Light is certainly a significant part of this garden, this landscape,' agreed Troy, when I asked him about it. 'I think Vita and Harold saw the light over Sissinghurst right, even right at the start, in the 1930s, and planned much of the garden around it. There are certain times of the year when the sun comes directly through the front arch, the tower, and the rose arbour in the White Garden at just the right angle. There is even a Lutyens bench in the Rose Garden that has been positioned to catch the light in the late afternoon. Harold liked to sit on this bench to watch the afternoon light. I don't think that's random. I think Harold was very aware of where the light travelled through the garden during the day and designed aspects of the garden rooms and their elements around it.'

Troy also believes that, along with light, the element of *genius loci* – or what gardeners and landscapers call the 'spirit of place' – is an integral part of Sissinghurst's atmosphere. 'Oh, the *genius loci* here is very much part of the garden,' he said, nodding enthusiastically. In contemporary garden design, *genius loci* refers to a location's distinctive atmosphere, although in ancient times it referred more to the protective spirit of a place. There are different meanings, but they are all part of the overarching definition: the 'spirit' of a landscape. Vita clearly observed these qualities in Sissinghurst. Many years later, in her book *English Country Houses*, written in 1941 for the 'Britain at War' series of patriotic books, she would write about this very thing. She even called it the 'spirit of place'. She referred to Knole, her childhood home, but she also mentioned many great houses that sit, deep-rooted, in their landscapes. She then said: 'the spirit of the place is very strong at Sissinghurst.'

Many landscapes resonate with us, sometimes for reasons we cannot explain. It might be the topography, the light of the day, the colour palette or planting scheme, or just the resplendent sight of rows of glorious flowers swaying before us. Often the beauty is overwhelming. Great garden designers try to create gardens that move people's emotions. Sissinghurst does this. Decades after Vita and Harold's death, the *genius loci* is still at work here.

'Very much so,' confirmed Troy, who says that he has even compiled an in-house *genius loci* guide for all the gardeners at Sissinghurst, which outlines each of the garden rooms and their atmosphere, their mood and their 'feel', and even the colour palettes for the plants and planting schemes. 'It articulates the vision for the garden,' he says. 'It helps me to understand what to do, now and in the future.'

A gardening friend of mine once told me about the curious term that Celts call 'thin places'. 'A thin place', he explained, was an old Celtic word to describe 'somewhere you experience sights so magnificent they transport you to a higher level'. It was, he said, a kind of transcendent experience that fuses the emotional, physical and mystical. He said it often happens when people are in gardens. Sissinghurst has the feeling of a thin place. There is a feeling of otherworldliness about it.

As I looked again at the pages of Vita's album, I turned back to the photo of Vita dressed in her beloved jodhpurs, with her knee-high boots – which she had started to wear to protect her legs when clearing thorns and nettles. She looked as strong as a spade. Ready for anything. Whatever Vita saw in the shell of Sissinghurst when she first inspected it in the rain on Friday, 4 April 1930, it was clear in this photo that she had not only a vision but also the fortitude to see it through.

What Vita could not have predicted, as she reluctantly posed for a photo in this optimistic spring of 1930, was how influential the garden would be, not only on her own life and that of Harold's but also on the worlds of horticulture, roses, and indeed the history of England itself, right through to the next century. Moreover, Sissinghurst would soon be the site of an incredible story involving roses, war, fortitude, love, and one woman's determination to ignore the Germans flying overhead by focusing on the beauty beneath her feet.

As the visitors to Sissinghurst started to crowd the paths, I closed the photo albums, took one last look out of the window of this tiny upstairs room, whispered my thanks to the spirits that may have been lingering, and walked away from 1930 and out into the bright autumn sunlight, to wander through the last of the late season roses before I made my way back to London.

I had a story about roses to research.

2

Old Roses for a New Garden

'Sissinghurst was to be a rose garden above all. But these would not be any roses. It would be a garden chiefly of "old roses", of the sort that a select group of horticultural connoisseurs were beginning to appreciate over and above the rather gaudy and too-perfect modern hybrids.'

Tim Richardson, *Sissinghurst: The Dream Garden*

Vita Sackville-West made an offer for Sissinghurst, which was accepted on 6 May 1930, a month after they had first inspected the property. Along with the estate, she bought the adjoining Victorian farmhouse and the 500-acre farm. She and Harold let the farm, known as 'Castle Farm', to Oswald Beale – the brother of Mr Beale, the land agent who had sold them the property. Oswald, or 'Ozzie', would come to be a steadfast friend for the rest of their lives. Harold, for all his new enthusiasm, was still fearful that they could not afford it. He was always conscious of money, but particularly now. In 1930, he had just resigned from his work as a diplomat in the Foreign Office and returned to England to take up the role of London Diarist at the *Evening Standard,* which did not pay much but gave him a voice in the media. Harold fretted about the cost of everything and for good reason. The garden at Sissinghurst would come to be one of the biggest costs in the couple's annual expenditure, and indeed their lives.

Vita returned to Sissinghurst in the days after the contract was signed, eager to begin work. Harold, too, was keen to get on. As most people who have been to Sissinghurst or have read something of its history know, it was Harold who masterminded its design, expertly connecting each of the awkwardly shaped garden rooms with linear paths, hedges and lines of sight that linked the garden in a pleasing way. It was a long, drawn-out process, which began with a mammoth clear-out of debris. Vita later recalled, in 1950 (*House & Garden*): 'It took three years to clear away the rubbish, three solid years, employing only an old man and his son who also had other jobs to do. It was not until 1933 that any serious planting could be undertaken.'

It was not an easy garden to design, wrote Vita. 'We had so very little to go on', she later recalled. Fortunately, Harold possessed 'enough ingenuity, and also enough large paper sheets ruled into squares, to grapple with the difficulties'.

Whenever I see a garden plan of Sissinghurst, with its imperfect perfection, I wonder if Harold Nicolson would do anything differently if he and Vita had bought Sissinghurst today? What would he have made of using Google Earth to map a place from space? Would he be amazed by Google Earth's 3D capability? Would he have easily taken to AutoCAD for his drawing?

Throughout that first summer in 1930, Vita and Harold continued to visit Sissinghurst, staying at either The George in Cranbrook, which is still there, or The Bull in Sissinghurst village, which is now The Milk House – and a lovely place to stay. (The Three Horseshoes is another.) They picnicked in the garden, in-between restoration work and making plans. One photo in their archives shows Vita digging a border in the south-west corner of the Tower Lawn. There is no garden around her and only the barest hint of lawn. But she is not deterred. She has her spade, and she is determined to begin digging her first garden bed. Behind her, the wall is bare. It seems difficult to conceive now, given that most of the walls at Sissinghurst are covered with roses.

There were many reasons Vita was intent on buying Sissinghurst. One of them was that it had high walls, which Vita could see would be the perfect backdrop for a garden of old roses. Vita loved old roses. She loved their unruly hedgerow style, their scent, their ruffled forms, their curious names, the way they felt like velvet, the way their petals fell on the table after they had been in a vase for a few days. She even loved the alchemy: the process of efflorescence from bud to fully formed rose. To her, roses were just as interesting on the inside.

Vita planted her first rose at Sissinghurst on 6 May 1930, the day that she and Harold signed the contract to buy it. She planted 'Madame Alfred Carrière', which they later nicknamed 'Mrs Alfonso's Career' according to biographer Jane Brown, on the south face of the South Cottage. Over the years it grew so high that it quickly took over most of the south face of the house. Vita told the gardeners to train it around her bedroom window to allow scent into the room during the summer months. (Sadly, it has since died).

'Madame Alfred Carrière' is a particularly beautiful rose, white with a hint of pink – like a shy young girl blushing at a boy at a summer garden party or a village fête. It has a display of ruffled petals that begin their inflorescence in May in England and continue right through the autumn. Its beauty belies its strength and vigorous growth habit – it can easily reach seven metres (twenty-three feet) in height. The rose dates from 1879 and was named after the wife of Alfred Carrière, the chief editor of *La Revue Horticole*, a famous horticultural publication in France, founded in 1829. It was bred in France by Joseph Schwartz and described as 'worthless' by *Le Journal des Roses* when it was first released. However, by 1908 it was proclaimed to be the best white climbing rose by the National Rose Society of Great Britain. The Royal Horticultural Society gave it an Award of Garden Merit in 1993. It is still one of the most popular white climbing roses today.

Vita, with her mother Victoria, had visited the great garden designer Gertrude Jekyll and her garden at Munstead Wood some years earlier. Vita's earliest gardening notebook shows that she was listing and planting roses that Gertrude Jekyll was also using in her planting schemes at this time. However, Vita was more inspired by the writings and garden plantings of designer and writer William Robinson, whose book *The English Flower Garden* had been a bestseller some years before. William Robinson was a visionary in his thinking. Rebelling against the formality of Victorian gardens, he advocated a looser planting structure, a more natural look. He loved blossoming hedges, for example, whether of roses, sweetbriar or honeysuckle. He loved to see ramblers grown on the walls of a house. Vita was enthralled, and began to adopt many of his ideas.

Sissinghurst's garden of roses began to take shape.

3

The Society Florist

'Everything I do is connected to nature
in one way or another.'

Alexander McQueen

While Vita Sackville-West was beginning her new garden, another rose lover was also trying to establish hers. Constance Spry was looking for a new direction after many years working as a headmistress. After much consideration, she had decided to open a florist's shop. She soon found a small, nondescript site at 7 Belgrave Road, Pimlico, a backstreet not far from Buckingham Palace, where, in 1928, she raised her shiny new sign: FLOWER DECORATIONS.

Like Vita, Connie (as she became known in her circle of friends) was a gardener, a writer and a rosarian. She has been described as 'tough', 'funny' and 'full of energy', and she probably had to be, not only to stay one step ahead of Mother Nature and her seasonal variations but also to stay ahead of the constantly changing trends in flower arranging. She was a true visionary in this field. The garden writer Beverley Nichols once described modern-day flower arranging as 'pre-Spry' and 'post-Spry', which shows how influential Connie was to become in the floral trade. But Connie's style was not something you could isolate or recognise as a brand. Just as she liked to create new gardens in her life, she liked to turn flowers on their heads. Sometimes literally. She decided that her new boutique, 'Flower Decorations', would stand apart from other florists by offering whimsical, wondrous and startlingly original bouquets and displays. Connie sourced many of her flowers and foliage from the sides of country roads and fields. Her favourites included leaves, berries, seedheads and golden hops. She would often supplement them with fresh blooms from Covent Garden Market, so the bouquets had that just-plucked-from-the-garden look. It was a clever strategy. But it was also a necessity. The new businesswoman was, like all new businesswomen during this period of economic hardship, trying to be thrifty. It is not easy to create beauty from frugality, but Constance Spry somehow created magic from Mother Nature's neglected vegetation.

Connie's big break had come in 1927. At a luncheon one Sunday, she found herself seated next to a fellow aesthete, Sidney Bernstein, who was a friend of Connie's friend Marjorie Russell. Mr Bernstein, it turned out, was the owner of Granada Cinemas. He recognised Connie's amateur talents from the simple but chic arrangements she had made for the luncheon table, and referred her to his friend Norman Wilkinson, a theatre designer. Norman and Connie immediately hit it off. They shared a love of flowers, flower growing, gardening and antiques.

Norman decided to recommend her to the royal perfumer Atkinsons, where he was designing the interiors. Atkinsons was updating its brand, having recently moved into a beautiful new building on the corner of Old Bond Street and Burlington Gardens in London. Connie's brief was clear: find and use flowers that reflect the old herbalists and perfumeries. (This was decades before beauty brands such as Aesop and other companies would adopt the same marketing strategies, thinking outside the box to create pared-back, natural-looking displays of foliage for their marketing and merchandising campaigns.) Connie returned with the bold suggestion of wild flowers and brambles from the hedgerows grown along the sides of roads and fields, which would look more 'natural' and possibly hint at the origins of the perfumes. She then suggested these be mixed with something 'up-market' – chartreuse-green cymbidium orchids, perhaps – to appeal to the more traditional client. To her surprise, Norman Wilkinson and Atkinsons agreed. She enhanced the flowers with antique containers, which she would continue to use all her life. She was inspired, she later said, by seventeenth- and eighteenth-century Dutch flower painters. (The biographer Diana Souhami revealed that Connie had once had an affair with the painter Gluck, born Hannah Gluckstein, which informed her floral style.) Atkinsons' display was an ingenious merchandising strategy. To passers-by, the displays looked as though they had come straight from the flower room of a country house, slightly dishevelled but beautiful in their fresh, natural state.

Connie's radical floral arrangements for Atkinsons entranced Mayfair's discerning browsers. According to Sue Shephard, author of the fascinating and inspirational biography *The Surprising Life of Constance Spry*, no one going up and down Bond Street on the dark winter nights of 1929 could possibly miss the thrilling, spotlit windows. Constance Spry was soon socialising among London's artistic set, including the interior decorator Syrie Maugham. She also befriended and worked with the theatre designer Oliver Messel, whose mother, Maud Messel, was another great advocate of old roses at this time. In time, Connie developed working friendships with many of these great names, as well as other leading creatives such as Norman Hartnell and Rex Whistler.

(Side note: there is a lot of information about Connie's early life and career in the archives of the RHS Lindley Library, where her personal papers are kept. There are also some wonderful stories about her in Sue Shephard's biography, as well as in an earlier, equally compelling biography by Elizabeth Coxhead. This book won't delve into Connie's early years as they have been covered extensively by these fine writers.)

Connie's partner at this time was a man called Henry Ernest Spry, or 'Harry' as he was often known, although Connie and his friends nicknamed him 'Shav'. (They never married, although Harry allowed Connie to use his surname.) Harry had been working in India for a period, but when he returned to England he decided to retrain as an accountant. One day, Shav found Connie going through her accounts, weeping with frustration. He was shocked to find that while selling cut flowers and making floral arrangements paid good money, much of the profit went on Connie's travel and expenses for more elaborate jobs for wealthier clients, jobs she seemed to be underquoting on. The couple wondered what to do to turn a financial corner. Connie, always ambitious, suggested they move the business. So, in 1934, they took on a lease for a building at 64 South Audley Street, in Mayfair. The location, argued Connie, would draw a more high-society clientele and she could therefore charge more. She also knew she would need more staff. And stylish uniforms to clothe them. Soon, preparations were being put in place for the design of the new premises, as well as the uniforms, which Victor Stiebel was commissioned to make.

In the next few years, Connie's business rapidly expanded. By 1939 she had 70 assistants working in various 'flower departments' – departments for boutonnières and corsages, for hats, for day and evening dresses and, of course, for fresh bouquets. A floral design school, books, and eventually a country retreat educating young women in the art of floristry, gardening and other home arts would follow.

Constance Spry was on her way to being the floral empress of London.

In 2021, amid the Covid pandemic years, the Garden Museum in London courageously staged an exhibition of Constance Spry's life, entitled 'Constance Spry and the Fashion for Flowers'. Shane Connolly, a renowned floral designer who designs flower arrangements for royal occasions as Connie had done, curated the exhibition, which made use of the extensive collection of her personal papers and records in the Royal Horticultural Society's Lindley Library. It was a tricky year to stage an exhibition, but perhaps it was perfectly timed, too: people longed to be free of lockdowns, and to see beauty and nature again.

To coincide with the exhibition, the *London Review of Books* published an article chronicling Connie's career and explaining how the headmistress-turned-businesswoman considered herself as much of a gardener as an entrepreneur. These horticultural skills, said the *London Review of Books*, were integral to her new role. Connie knew flowers; she knew their growing seasons; their faults and strengths; whether they drooped soon after they had been picked; the other plants and foliage they paired well with. 'I was first, and hope last to be, a gardener,' she wrote years later. According to the *London Review of Books*, 'by the time [Connie] opened her first shop, in Belgrave Road, she was already a knowledgeable plantswoman, with an important collection of old roses.' Along with her contemporaries, including Graham Stuart Thomas and Vita Sackville-West, Constance Spry would prove to be one of the rose world's most important guardians, safeguarding the survival of old roses throughout the twentieth century.

I was intrigued by Miss Constance Spry and wanted to find out more. So, on a perfect autumn day in early October 2022, a day so warm that many Londoners had removed their coats and found a park to sit in with their faces to the sun, I took the Tube to Green Park and walked to 24 Old Bond Street to find the former site of Atkinsons perfumery, where Connie had her first flower arranging job. I stopped at the corner of Old Bond Street and Burlington Gardens and I looked up: it was now a Salvatore Ferragamo store. Directly opposite was Ralph Lauren's London flagship store, where people sat and drank expensive smoothies from the Ralph Lauren café, and on the other side of Bond Street was Alexander McQueen's sleek boutique. Despite these changes in the urban landscape, I could imagine Atkinsons' windows in all their Constance Spry finery, and how, when they were lit at night, passers-by on Bond Street would have stopped and stared. Nonetheless, a part of me was disappointed. I do not know what I expected. Perhaps I expected something that looked like Wild at Heart, the wildly romantic florist that wows instagrammers in Notting Hill and once dominated Pimlico Road in Belgravia. (Later I walked to 64 South Audley Street, where Connie moved her business, and found the English Heritage plaque commemorating her legacy: *Constance Spry – Designer in Flowers – worked here.*)

After I stood for a while and imagined the glamour of Atkinsons, I crossed the road and stood outside the Alexander McQueen boutique. I had heard about a remarkable exhibition called 'Roses' that was being shown in its exhibition space. A friend had urged me to visit. It was, she said, 'extraordinary'. So I entered and climbed the sculptural spiral staircase to the upstairs gallery. What I did not expect, when I reached the top floor, was that an enormous wall of photographs of Sissinghurst Garden would await me. And that I would spend the next two hours immersed in a modern world of old roses.

Everything in Alexander McQueen's exhibition space that day paid homage to roses. The gallerist Hannah told me that McQueen's then Creative Director, Sarah Burton, and the entire design team at McQueen, including the Head of Atelier Judy Halil, took a weekend out of their lives several times a year and went on field trips to gardens to find botanical inspiration in the English landscape – just as Constance Spry had done. For one of their recent research trips, Hannah said, the team had travelled to Sissinghurst and other country gardens in Kent, including Vita's former homes at Knole and Long Barn, where the designers were inspired by the plantings, the perennial flowers and the roses. 'You can see how the collections have evolved from these outings in nature,' explained Hannah. I told her that I was writing a book about old roses, and that it included Sissinghurst, and she looked at me with delight. For the next two hours, Hannah and I talked about nothing but roses.

The McQueen exhibition was an ode to roses in all their forms. It included dresses and gowns from McQueen's floral-inspired collections as well as pieces from Sarah Burton. There was a dress that looked like a garden, which she and her atelier team had 'cultivated' on the model, sewing fabric flowers to look as if they were naturally growing up the dress, seeded from English country-house flower beds. There was a dress designed to resemble a gigantic rose, created by draping a single piece of silk taffeta, round and round, like the petals of a grand old red rose. There were corsets embroidered with roses using elegant needlepoint, and a fascinating wall of masterfully made fabric roses. And there were exquisite dresses made from petal-pink silk tulle and washed taffeta strewn with tumbling garlands of roses, with several roses hanging freely from the hem. 'Isn't it beautiful?' said Hannah, indicating the dress I was staring at, transfixed. 'The design team were going to snip those extra roses dangling from the hem, as they were simply extraneous, but Sarah Burton said no, reasoning that you would not prune a rose simply because it was dangling over a garden path.'

The most poetic 'rose' dress in the exhibition was 'Sarabande', the name given to the gown that closed McQueen's Spring/Summer 2007 show at the Paris Cirque d'Hiver. To create this piece, McQueen asked florist Phyllida Holbeach to find fresh roses – many of them old roses – in muted shades of purple, dusty pink and sage green. These roses and flowers were then semi-frozen and flown to Paris, where the seamstresses (*petites mains*) finished sewing them on to the outfit barely an hour before the model walked on to the catwalk. 'When the model appeared on the stage, however, the fresh roses and flowers began to defrost and fall off,' said Hannah.' 'Roses scattered on the catwalk. The audience thought it was deliberate, and gasped, and then applauded with joy.' Backstage, Alexander McQueen was moved by the crowd's applause. He was so touched by the reaction that he later named his charity the Sarabande Foundation, after the show. The 'rose' dress that closed the show became known as the 'Sarabande dress' and has travelled the world in many McQueen exhibitions. In-between viewings, it has been restored more than nine times, as the real roses and flowers were replaced with silk and fabric versions. During one of the restorations, however, the designers made the poignant discovery that a single tiny rosebud had survived on the dress.

The Alexander McQueen team has kept the old rosebud safe, as a small memento of that extraordinary show.

Vita would have loved this Roses exhibition. She once wrote that roses should be approached as though they were textiles rather than flowers. She loved the roses that looked like velvet, the ones with 'richness and grandeur', as she described them. Vita particularly loved 'Charles de Mills', which has the texture and layers of a crimson-pink velvet coat, like a wonderful outfit you would wear to the opera, folding over itself as you walked up the stairs to be seated for Act One.

As the afternoon shadows drew longer, I knew I had to leave this splendid exhibition of roses and gowns and make my way back to my tiny hotel in Belgravia. I told Hannah how grateful I was for her company and her wonderful stories, and how privileged I felt to see it.

I was also more determined than ever to find out how Vita and Connie helped save old roses during one of the most turbulent periods of horticultural and political history.

4

The Young Rosarian

'To garden is to impose order. It is the conquest
of nature, the harnessing of nature to a purpose,
initially practical and later aesthetic.'

Penelope Lively, *Life in the Garden*

Eighty miles or so north-west from Sissinghurst, two hours by car across the Thames estuary and through the quiet Essex countryside towards Cambridge, past Ellen Willmott's once-magnificent garden and estate at Warley Place, which was slowly deteriorating and would soon be a ruin, another ambitious gardener and future rosarian was also finding his way.

Graham Stuart Thomas was celebrating his twenty-first birthday on 3 April 1930, the same week that Vita found Sissinghurst. Graham did not know it as he toasted the day with family and friends but he was on his way to becoming one of the greatest rosarians England has known. As the journalist James Fenton later wrote in *The Guardian* on 13 September 2003: 'Few plantsmen could better the sheer expertise of Graham Stuart Thomas, guardian of old rose varieties. He was a key figure in the preservation [of them].' The *New York Times* was similarly salutary in its obituary of Graham on 28 April 2003. Graham Stuart Thomas, it declared, was 'the single most influential figure in preserving the horticultural heritage of the [British] nation'.

Despite Graham Stuart Thomas's long career and lasting horticultural legacy, little has been written about him. Many knowledgeable garden writers and journalists have written articles about him for magazines and newspapers, but there is certainly not the volume you would expect for a horticulturist of his fame. I have researched him for several years, spending hours in the RHS Lindley Library, buying his books and reading articles, but I still do not feel that I know who he is. He is an enigma.

So I wrote to someone who might know more about the mystery of Mr Thomas.

Charles Quest-Ritson and his wife, Brigid, are the authors of the *RHS Encyclopedia of Roses*. Charles was a director of the Royal National Rose Society and a founder of the Historic Roses Group. Charles and Brigid are working on their own study of Graham, which pleases me because he is long overdue a biography. In June 2023, Charles and Brigid kindly allowed me to visit them at their home in a tiny village near Wilton in Wiltshire.

I asked them about their friendship with Graham Stuart Thomas and the first thing Charles did was correct me on his name. 'For a start, it is not Graham Stuart Thomas. It is just Graham Thomas,' said Charles. 'He added the 'Stuart' in the middle of his name to make it sound more upper class.' 'Oh,' I said, momentarily displaced, and made a note. 'Well, let's just call him Graham, then,' I suggested. I could see it was going to be an interesting discussion.

'Vita was intensely romantic, but she was also an intellectual who was educated in classical languages and history,' explains Charles. 'That's probably why she loved old roses, because of their romance and stories and history. But Graham was a businessman, a clever one. He promoted old roses for a different reason – money.' Sensing this could be an afternoon of memorable bon mots, I began writing. 'Graham's interest in roses really stemmed from his boss, Thomas Hilling. Graham worked for Thomas Hilling at Hilling's Nursery. And it was Thomas Hilling who first identified that there could be a demand for old roses. The plan to propagate and sell old roses was a joint effort between Thomas and Graham.'

Graham, explained Charles, was extremely clever. 'He was aware of the power of myth and self-promotion. He knew he could create a market for old roses. He knew that people would think they were rare and special and beautiful. Taste comes from the top down, so he appealed to the upper classes first. Then he marketed and sold the old roses for a high price.' That's how he came to be associated with them, said Charles. He was not romantic, like Vita. He was not a conservationist who wanted to save them, although later he may have been aware that he played a part in their survival. He was a hard-headed businessman. And that businessman made it his business to source, propagate and sell rare and old roses. But surely he was passionate about them, too? Surely he was a gardener at heart? 'Of course!' said Charles. 'But he was also very ambitious.'

Graham, I learned during this interview, and in the weeks afterwards as I continued my research, was motivated to succeed. In the same month that Vita bought Sissinghurst, Graham was working for the Cambridge University Botanic Garden, tending to the new plants being sent back to England by explorers on plant-hunting expeditions. He later told the *New York Times* that he had 'apprenticed himself' to the Cambridge University Botanic Garden in return for an education. After two-and-a-half years, however, Graham was restless and began considering his next career move. He needed, he felt, a business education. So, in early 1930 he gave notice, packed up his garden tools, and began work at Six Hills Nursery in Stevenage, a well-known nursery with a good reputation. Working under noted plantsman Clarence Elliott, Graham built on his practical and theoretical knowledge. However, Graham only stayed at Six Hills for less than a year. He contracted scarlet fever, and had to be admitted to hospital. After a few weeks away from work, he was fired. Once he had recovered, he found a new role at T. Hilling & Co. (often shortened to Hillings), a three hundred-acre wholesale nursery near Chobham in Surrey. He remained at Hillings until 1955, and worked his way up from foreman to manager.

I told Charles that I had become confused by many aspects of Graham's life during the research process. I said that I had noticed a lot of inconsistences. It happens to all biographers – stories are told and retold, and by the time they appear somewhere a fifth or sixth or tenth time, the truth has blurred. But in Graham's case, I said, the stories of his life – the dates, the details – had become so indistinct at times, it was difficult to know where the truth ended and the myth of the man began. He was clearly a great horticulturist, but I could not understand his character, his motivations, his ambitions. 'Well, Graham was adept at self-promotion,' explained Charles. Did he ever embellish his stories? 'He certainly knew the power of a good story.'

I was mystified by this. Here was a man who was shy, who was reticent about revealing his private life – 'he did not talk about himself much,' offered Charles, 'and almost never about his friends' – yet he was also adept at self-promotion. And he was clearly ambitious – a workaholic with grace and good manners who learned how to liaise with all classes – but he was also quiet, contemplative, almost analytical, with a fine business mind. What motivated him, I wondered?

I spent several hours with the Quest-Ritsons, but jetlag and travel fatigue forced me to shut my notebook and thank them for their time. I suspected I would need to talk to them again. There was far too much to cover in a single afternoon. I checked into a hotel in Wilton for the evening and continued researching Graham's life. The next day, I decided to visit Mottisfont Abbey, Graham's great masterpiece of a garden, which holds the national collection of old-fashioned roses, known formally as the National Collection of Pre-1900 Shrub Roses.

(Side story: on a visit Sissinghurst in 2022, head gardener Troy Scott Smith told me that he recalled meeting Graham – who is his hero – at Sissinghurst when Troy was twenty-one. 'It was probably 1992 or 1993; I was just starting out as a gardener and working at Sissinghurst,' Troy explained to me. 'Graham was quiet, professional and well-dressed, with a brown jacket on. He came through the arch at Sissinghurst and stopped near the Purple Border. It was autumn, and we spoke for half an hour or so. He was very kind to even talk to me, given how famous he was.' Troy could not offer much more. It was, he said, a fleeting meeting.)

Mottisfont is only a half an hour away from Wilton, where I was staying. It was Sunday, so I knew it would be busy. But I hoped that if I arrived early enough, I would miss the crowds. I was wrong. Mottisfont has had a makeover in recent years, with a fancy new entrance to the grounds. Consequently, it is inundated with visitors and now suffers from the same thing Sissinghurst does – popularity. I loved the old Mottisfont, but I understand that places need to evolve to survive. As many of the old roses here only flower once and June is when they peak, June is the best month to visit. But it is also the busiest month. (Tip: the garden is open late most nights during June, so evening is a great time to visit to avoid the crowds. It is also the best time to smell the roses' scent.)

Mottisfont's walled garden of roses is Graham Thomas's legacy, his gift to the world. There are walls and walls of incredible Noisettes and Climbing Tea roses, Wichurana and Multiflora ramblers, China roses, Scots roses, a few Rugosa hybrids and Bourbon roses. There are Gallicas, Damasks, Albas and Centifolias, plus a sprinkling of Portland roses. Most of them are pink, lilac and purple shades, which look like a magnificent *millefleur* in a certain light. If you love roses, particularly old roses, this is a garden you must see. 'Mottisfont is the best garden in Britain to learn about old roses,' Charles had told me, so I spent the afternoon wandering the paths, bending and inspecting, bending and inspecting. I studied the enormous Gallica roses, with their remarkable scents. I took in the Damask roses in their shades of pink or white. I felt the Moss roses, with their soft textures. And I searched for the most beautiful Bourbons and Noisettes. Everything was laid out so that visitors could study and compare the different varieties. Almost every rose had an identifying tag, so visitors could write down its name. It was, as Charles said, an astonishing education. The ruffled glamour and grace of these lovely roses was so memorable that I can still recall them today. I thought about what John Wood, head gardener at the National Trust property Hinton Ampner, had told me in 2022. 'What Graham Stuart Thomas achieved at Mottisfont is underrated. Most people have no idea how incredible it is.'

I interviewed John Wood in October 2022, after travelling to Hinton Ampner to see him. Hinton Ampner is a must-see for gardeners: the walled garden of flowers, roses and fruits is glorious and the enormous rose beds at the front are splendid, even in late summer. John has worked for the National Trust for twenty-five years, but his formative years were spent at Mottisfont, assisting with the restoration of the garden and its roses. 'I grew up in the area around Mottisfont and used to see its then head gardener, David Stone, walking to work each day. I used to think "it's just a walled garden; what does he do all day?" One day, I met David in the pub. He told me he wanted someone to do some double digging [a technique that involves turning soil over to the depth of two spade heads]. I said I would do it, and so I became a gardener.'

John told me he met Graham a few times when he visited Mottisfont – 'although', he corrected himself, 'the gardeners did not really "meet" Graham ... only the senior garden consultants at the Trust had that privilege.' John said Graham was in his eighties by the time John was working at Mottisfont, yet Graham was as observant as ever and noticed everything, no matter how small. All gardeners are like that, I suggested. Yes, nodded John, but Graham was particularly sharp. 'Graham used to visit Mottisfont to see how the roses were going. It would be announced that he was visiting, and we would make sure the garden was immaculate for his visit. Graham – although you never called him Graham; it was always Mr Thomas – did not speak directly to the gardeners. He always walked around with one of the Trust's garden consultants, looking at everything with a close eye. Afterwards, we – the gardeners – would receive his feedback. One year, the head gardener David Stone had planted alliums and David later heard from the Trust person that Graham did not like them in his rose beds. "There are too many onions!" Graham said. "It is not an *onion patch*, Mr Stone!"' John Wood laughed as he recounted the story. 'Graham Stuart Thomas had lost sight in one eye by then, I think, but he was still as observant as ever!'

I asked John what he thought of Mottisfont, of its significance as a garden. He thought about the question before answering. 'I don't think people understand how unique Mottisfont's collection of old roses is. In the past, Mottisfont's visitors were mostly rosarians and connoisseurs of roses. Now it is families who want a fun day out. Most of these visitors aren't rose people, who know about old roses. It is wonderful that they want to come and have fun, but I worry about the roses. There are some very important, very rare roses there, roses that aren't found anywhere else. Graham used to propagate them, to preserve them. And he used the original stock, too. What he achieved at Mottisfont is underrated, I think. Most people have no idea how incredible it is. I just think it would be great to educate more people about the significance of the garden.'

John paused, as if to consider his next words. 'It concerns me that the age of the average rose grower, and particularly those who love heritage roses, is getting older. Soon that knowledge will die out. And many of the old roses may die too. Even the main rose nurseries are thinning down their catalogues. The three biggest rose suppliers and rose breeders in England are Peter Beales, Trevor White and David Austin, and one of these is already downsizing its collection of old roses. People do not understand how beautiful heritage old roses can be. They do not realise the intensity of colour, or the history each rose has. These old roses are often lost to the world, and without people like Graham Stuart Thomas even more old roses would be lost. If we are lucky, some of them can still be found in gardens and hedgerows and saved. Some of the grander English gardens are reinstating their old roses. Morden

Hall Park, south of Wimbledon, is one. Sissinghurst is another. But we need to do more to save them. If we do not, there is a good chance they will die out.'

Which is exactly what Vita, Constance and, yes, Graham and several others realised, in the middle of the twentieth century.

5

The Aristocratic
Rose Collector

'All the great twentieth-century gardens were exercises in
garden history, brimming with nostalgia for a lost time.'

Katherine Swift

While Vita Sackville-West, Constance Spry and Graham Stuart Thomas were establishing their new careers, their new lives and their new gardens, one aristocrat was already settling into hers.

Maud Messel was an important member of one of Britain's most notable design and gardening families in the early part of the twentieth century, yet little is known about her achievements. More is known about the rose garden she created at Nymans in southern England in the 1920s and 1930s. A little more is known about her son, Oliver Messel, one of the leading theatre and interior designers for much of the twentieth century. And even more is known about her grandson, the photographer Antony Armstrong-Jones (later Earl of Snowdon), who married the Queen's sister, Princess Margaret. Yet these two owe much of their design DNA to their mother and grandmother. Maud Messel was one of the most artistic, most creative women of her day. And in 1930, her rose garden at Nymans was regarded by experts as being one of the most significant collections of old roses in England. It was a floral tribute to a wealthy aristocrat who – like Vita – did not need to work but did, who did not need to garden but did, and who did not need to care about growing roses when she had gardeners to do it for her, but still did.

Maud Messel was raised in London in the late 1800s, as the daughter of the celebrated *Punch* cartoonist Edward Linley Sambourne. She spent her childhood in one of the most incredible houses in London, 18 Stafford Terrace, Kensington (now the Sambourne House museum). In 1898, at the age of twenty-three and after a dazzling few years dancing around London as one of the city's most stunning debutantes, she settled down with the stockbroker Leonard Messel.

In the first years of their marriage Leonard and Maud resided in an elegant white stuccoed mansion at 104 Lancaster Gate, overlooking the leafy splendour of Hyde Park. There, her three children were born in quick succession: Linley, Anne and Oliver. The family loved London life, but Maud longed for a garden. She and Leonard soon found and purchased a country property called Balcombe House, in West Sussex. Maud's father-in-law, Ludwig, a successful stockbroker, also wanted a country garden. Some years earlier, in 1890, he had purchased a country property called Nymans on six hundred acres in the nearby village of Handcross. There, with his gardener James Comber, he began to create a magnificent Arts and Crafts-inspired garden, where sculptural topiary framed astonishing new plants collected from around the world. Both Maud and her father-in-law settled happily into their country lives and gardens – Maud at Balcombe and Ludwig at Nymans.

When Ludwig died in 1915, Maud and Leonard inherited Nymans, and the garden that Ludwig had carefully planted became theirs. (The impressive development of Nymans under Ludwig's ownership is chronicled in the compelling books, *Nymans: The Story of a Sussex Garden* by Shirley Nicholson, and *From Refugees to Royalty* by John Hilary.)

Like Vita, Maud was a romantic and wanted a house she could embroider with roses. Ludwig's was not a house, Maud felt, that was suited to roses. So, in the 1920s, two architects in succession were employed to create an enchanting new stone mansion. According to Nymans' Cultural Heritage Curator, Caroline Ikin, Maud had a clear vision. She wanted a romantic house. And she wanted roses – lots of them – climbing up the walls. She wanted them to form part of the architecture, just as Vita envisaged at Sissinghurst. Maud was soon determined to have one of the most idyllic rose gardens in England, filled with mostly older varieties. Maud's father-in-law had already planted many old roses at Nymans, but Maud added to these by organising for her favourite roses to be uprooted and brought over from Balcombe.

Maud then set her sights on sourcing as many old roses as she could find. This is when she and Leonard began travelling abroad on their botanical adventures.

According to Caroline Ikin, Maud and Leonard became interested in seed collecting, and travelled to Europe, usually in the spring, to find new plants and seeds. The Messels were amateurs to begin with (in that they were not professional botanists), but their enthusiasm put them on a par with professionals, and they soon acquired both extensive botanical knowledge and many rare plants from all their travels. The Messels embarked on seed-collecting missions to Italy and the south of France, sending back plants to expand their collection at Nymans, and also to the Royal Botanic Gardens at Kew. They were particularly involved in the search for old roses. They were also conservationists – they kept one plant of everything that they collected overseas, in the greenhouses at Nymans, in order to create a kind of 'library' of all their precious plants. One of the pages in Maud's garden diaries shows how many plants, including roses, she and Leonard collected on their travels. In March 1930, Maud wrote: Sent Comber [head gardener] many baskets of cuttings and plants from Mentone, San Remo, Argentine Valley, Florence and surrounding country.

Many of the roses Maud found on her travels in Italy and France were the old varieties. Maud was particularly fond of old roses with gentle colours, usually pastel shades, such as pink. The writer and rose enthusiast Dr J. Elizabeth Perks wrote about Nymans for a research paper (provided for this book by Nymans and the National Trust), for which she used research and writings by Graham Stuart Thomas, Stephen Lacey, Shirley Nicholson and Michael Gibson. According to Elizabeth, Maud acquired some of her old roses from Ellen Willmott, the notable rosarian and owner of Warley Place in Essex (now a ruin), who had written an illustrated book about roses called *The Genus Rosa*. She would also come to know Graham Stuart Thomas, too, as well as the nurseryman Edward Bunyard, from whom she ordered roses in 1934, according to her diary entries. (More on Edward Bunyard later.) These gardening friends and rose enthusiasts contributed significantly to both Maud's growing collection and her expanding knowledge of roses, although she also continued her 'rose expeditions', searching for rare roses and other plants in Europe. With these expeditions, and these friendships, Maud's rose garden quickly became a showpiece. As Graham Stuart Thomas later wrote of one of his visits to Nymans, 'The old varieties were especially treasured by Mrs Messel, and hours were spent turning the pages of Redouté's great volumes, trying to identify some of the roses that had reached the gardens from various sources.' Graham himself later identified some of the unnamed roses in Maud's rose garden, such as 'Blush Noisette'. He later wrote that although he had seen this rose now and then in old gardens through England, he had not met anyone who had an inkling of its name and history. Other roses that Graham identified included 'Aimée Vibert', a white Noisette with crimson buds that looks as if it belongs in a painting (1828) and 'Fellemberg' (1835), which is a mid-pink, almost cerise. (Side note: it is always worth looking at the two sides of rose petals. They are seldom of exactly the same colour, tint or shade. 'Fellemberg' is an example of a rose with dark pink petal backs but paler pink inner petals.)

In his fine book *The Rose Gardens of England* (1988), Michael Gibson recalled many of the roses he himself found at Nymans in the 1980s, including a rambler at the entrance to the rose garden called 'Princesse Marie', and various Gallicas, Damasks, Centifolias and Albas. He also listed several roses of special interest because they were rare and hardly ever seen in modern gardens, including 'Lady Curzon', 'Sissinghurst Castle', 'René André', 'Cerise Bouquet', 'Honorine de Brabant' (now identified as 'Gros Provins Panaché', a wonderfully speckled pink-and-white rose, like an Impressionist painting), 'The Chestnut Rose' (*R. roxburghii*), 'The White Rose of York" ('Alba Semi-Plena'), and 'Maiden's Blush' ('Cuisse de Nymphe').

It needs to be stated that these roses could have been planted by Maud Messel, or they could have been added to the garden after she died, continuing the tradition of growing beautiful and unusual roses at Nymans. As Charles Quest-Ritson points out, there have been several restorations and replantings of the rose garden at Nymans over the years.

The rose garden reached its peak of beauty in the 1930s, just as Vita and Harold were establishing their own rose collection at Sissinghurst. In fact, these fruitful years were the beginning of an intense period of creativity for Maud, in gardening but also in other areas, such as textiles, embroidery, fashion (her flower-inspired gowns were legendary) and interior design. According to Thomas Messel, who wrote about Maud in his biography *Oliver Messel: In the Theatre of Design*, Maud's ability to beautify the spaces around her, her knowledge of plants and horticulture, her endless creativity, and her practical skills in not only gardening but also drawing, needlework and design had a long-lasting effect on all her family. The Messel family, led by Maud, surrounded themselves by beauty of every kind, from art to textiles, furniture, fashion and flowers.

These years following the First World War but before the Second World War were a period in which people sought to create a new, beautiful and beguiling world; an idyll of flowers, roses and English romanticism, even if it was being planted in the shadow of Hitler's growing dominance. Roses were one way for people to forget what was happening in Europe. They represented everything that was good and beautiful about England. They were the quintessence of Englishness.

On a beautiful spring day in 2022, against a gentle sunrise that was the delicate pink of a 'Jacques Cartier' rose (my favourite rose, although its name is temporary until its real name is discovered), I took an early train to Crawley and then a taxi through the villages of West Sussex to see this 'ruin of roses' for myself. Nymans is not far from London – a quick hour on the train – but feels a century away. I was early, so I walked the garden paths, empty of visitors, and eventually it was time to meet Curator Dr Caroline Ikin, who kindly showed me the garden. It was the end of May, so the famous roses were not due to be in bloom but already they were putting on a spectacular show. England's garden season seems to begin earlier every year, but even so, I was surprised by the voluptuousness of both the buds and the open roses, which seemed to have more layers than one of Maud's famously sumptuous evening gowns. Clearly, I had arrived in precisely the right week.

In all my years of being a garden writer I have never seen a garden like Nymans, although I imagine Ninfa in Italy comes close. The most surprising thing is that there is no grand country house to speak of, just the dignified, ruined remains of one – although there are still a few liveable wings in the rear. It almost looks like an illusion, or a stage set, one designed by Oliver Messel himself. The windows are open to the sky and the grand stone walls have been left as they were after the fire in 1947 that destroyed the house, except that now there are roses climbing over them. In fact, while I loved the garden, it was the house in its romantic state, with climbing roses growing up the façade and through the hollow windows, that really appealed to my romantic's heart. It is a magical, atmospheric garden. The perfect garden of ruins and roses.

I should add that Nymans is also renowned for its camellias and rhododendrons. These, and the garden's rare trees and shrubs, are really the basis of its horticultural fame. Ludwig, Maud's father-in-law, created a magnificent garden long before Maud and Leonard inherited the property.

Nymans' rose garden contains mostly old varieties, as well as modern English roses and ramblers. There are both single blooms and densely petalled roses, repeat-flowering varieties, and those old roses that just flower once. The ramblers bloom once, in pendant sprays that cover the walls. May and June are the best time to see them. It is during these months that Nymans really feels like an enchanting, rose-covered idyll, lost to time.

There are more than six hundred roses at Nymans, and on this glorious spring day of my visit, when the flowers were heated gently by the sun, it seemed as if their scent carried all the way down the garden paths. I felt as though we could smell every single one. Exiting the house, I turned back, to take one last look at the ruins of Nymans, clothed in roses. It was an extraordinary scene.

6

Establishing Roots

(and a New Life)

'We need space that liberates us from terra firma, allowing our spirits to soar and our imaginations to take flight.'

Landscape and interior designer John Saladino

I t is easy to see how Vita could have been bewitched. The hard spring sunlight of early April 1930 may have shown every crack, but the height and magnificence of the tower was still something to behold. It offered an incredible view over the Kent countryside, and for Vita, searching for her home in this, her much-loved landscape, that view must have tugged at her romantic heart. However, Vita, for all her optimism, was pragmatic enough to realise that the property and its garden needed help. Even though Vita and Harold were financially stretched (it was only when Vita's mother died in 1936 that they had serious money), she decided they needed a team of gardeners to assist in the Herculean task of clearing centuries of debris. Two gardeners, George Hayter and his son Tom, were employed (the principal gardeners from 1930 to 1936), and a handyman/chauffeur, Jack Copper, was also taken on. They, and many other labourers who were happy to work during these post-Depression years, were soon busy clearing the estate. (Vita and Harold were not short of help: Sissinghurst's staff, according to Adam Nicolson, included a cook, a kitchen maid, a butler, a chauffeur and – by 1939 – four gardeners. Vita also employed, at various stages, a lady's maid and secretaries.)

One of the most curious things about Sissinghurst's garden is that it links the living spaces like a verdant, seasonally changing passageway. Vita and Harold always planned to have their living quarters in the South Cottage, which offered the couple two bedrooms, a bathroom, Harold's sitting room, a small 'bookroom' and a flower room. The kitchen and dining room were in the Priest's House, and Vita and Harold's sons also slept in the Priest's House when they were home from boarding school. The library was in the main house, which was where the housekeeper and cook slept. It was an unconventional arrangement, to have the children living apart from their parents - although their sons were away at boarding school for many years, so they were probably used to the separation. However, it also forced the family to use the garden several times a day, criss-crossing the paths to see each other and to dine and work and sleep. Even in the depths of winter snow they had to cross the garden paths to reach each building. And this is what, perhaps more than anything, transformed Sissinghurst. The garden became a green hall linking one living space to another, a conduit for the couple's energy as they strode along the pavers. Whether it was intended or not, the decision to use the garden and its connecting paths as another 'room' in their living spaces was an ingenious move. Sissinghurst soon came to life through its garden paths.

Vita's first night at Sissinghurst was on 16 October 1930. She slept on her own in the turret, with her two dogs Henry and Sarah beside her for company. There was no electricity, and the wind was howling outside, but she was determined to embrace her new home with all its cracks and creaks and groans. She taped up cardboard sheets to shield the windows from the rain and settled in to enjoy her new private idyll. Sissinghurst was never going to be a warm place to live. Adam Nicolson said Vita and Harold often endured extreme discomfort. One winter morning, Vita awoke to find a perfect counterpane of snow on her bed, which had come in through the roof during the night. Ursula Codrington, Vita's secretary, always maintained that every part of Sissinghurst was usually freezing: 'there was never any heating.'

The day after Vita's first night at Sissinghurst, Vita's friend Hilda Matheson visited. The two women spent the day gardening, edging paths and marking out the garden by the South Cottage. On Saturday 18 October 1930, it was Harold's turn to stay overnight, and he travelled down from London. Harold's first evening in their new home was not a happy one. Vita served sardines and tinned tongue for a 'picnic dinner' by candlelight in the South Cottage. The couple then retired to camp beds, reading by candlelight. Vita's dogs stayed by her side, keeping her warm. Harold was not as comfortable: 'I was very wet and very cold,' he said later. For future visits, he booked a room at the Bull Inn in the village, where he must have felt warmer and more comfortable.

In the final months of 1930, more furniture was moved from Long Barn to Sissinghurst. Once Harold knew the buildings were halfway habitable (and possibly the risk of suffering a damp camp bed was over), he, Vita and the boys slept at Sissinghurst on 6 December. But it would be two years before they could properly move into Sissinghurst, which Harold nicknamed 'Sissingbags'. The family would not move their final possessions until April 1932. In the meantime, they divided their time between Sissinghurst and Long Barn, although Harold spent weekdays in London while the boys were at boarding school. Vita, however, was happy to stay there on her own and continue work on the garden, especially her expanding rose garden.

Vita's daily routine rarely changed. Breakfast was served at nine – although often she would walk around the garden before it. After breakfast, she would reply to her letters, and then she would retreat to her tower to write. Lunch was at one, and Vita would take another stroll around the garden before the midday meal. Afternoons were for further writing. After tea, she would take the dogs for a long walk or work in the garden. She preferred to be in the garden in the quiet of the late afternoon, when the gardeners had left for the day. Often she wrote at night, too. It depended on her mood or the season.

As every month passed, Vita became more and more comfortable in her new life at Sissinghurst.

In a stroke of luck for Graham Stuart Thomas, Hillings nursery was located conveniently close to where the great garden designer Gertrude Jekyll lived and gardened at Munstead Wood. One of Graham's ambitions was to meet Miss Jekyll and so he wrote to her, asking if he could visit. He later wrote: 'On a warm Sunday afternoon, I cycled all the way through Guildford and Godalming to Munstead, a distance of about 15 miles.'

Gertrude Jekyll was an intimidating figure. Her professional partnership with the architect Sir Edwin Lutyens had given her a wide audience in the landscape architecture world but she was also respected in the gardening world for her planting prowess, for her books and for her journalism. Vita Sackville-West had also visited Gertrude Jekyll at Munstead Wood, together with Lutyens and Vita's mother, Victoria, on 25 August 1917. Walking through the garden at Munstead Wood, the twenty-five-year-old Vita was polite and deferential but not overly impressed. She later wrote that Gertrude Jekyll's garden was 'not at its best but one can see it must be lovely,' although, as it was late August at the time, it is understandable that she might have been underwhelmed. However, Vita does seem to have taken note of some aspects of the planting details.

It is not known what Graham and Miss Jekyll conversed about over tea that afternoon at Munstead Wood. Whatever it was, Gertrude Jekyll profoundly influenced Graham's views on flowers, roses and gardening in general. As the *Irish Times* later noted on 28 April 2003: 'Jekyll introduced him [Graham] to the garden as art.' Miss Jekyll showed Graham that plants could be used in a painterly arrangement, composed to create an impressionistic effect in the same way that oil paints could.

By August 1931, the area in front of the Priest's House at Sissinghurst had been cleared of debris, and Vita and Harold were now ready to begin marking it out as the site of a rose garden. (It is now the White Garden, the Rose Garden having been moved to the vegetable garden.) By September 1931, the couple had forged the paths and were ready to plant. Harold was meticulous by nature, and probably wanted to be sure of the garden design and planting scheme before committing to anything. Vita's talents were in design, in seeing how plants would look together and drawing up planting schemes. Some of the first roses for Sissinghurst's new garden were the Hybrid Tea 'Madame Edouard Herriot', the climbing form of 'Richmond' (on her tower) and 'Fortune's Double Yellow' (on the Bishopsgate wall). She also planted the rambler 'Albertine' to the right of the tower steps, where it entwines with 'Paul's Lemon Pillar' – both planted in the 1930s. Vita adored 'Paul's Lemon Pillar'. It reminded her of 'curled shavings of marble'. Most of all, she loved the petals that covered the ground like a Persian carpet.

While restoration work on Sissinghurst's buildings progressed, the garden began to emerge from the centuries of debris. Did Harold and Vita know how far they had come? How much they had achieved in such a short time? Or were they, like most people who renovate old houses and gardens, exhausted by the stress and complications and enormous cost of it all? They were still young enough to have the energy to undertake such an enormous restoration. But surely the work was taking its toll?

It was certainly taking up much of their finances. By 1932, the couple were living well beyond their means. Harold constantly fretted about money. He and Vita often had to make decisions about where to spend and where to save: 'We planted hornbeam where we could not afford yew,' Vita once wrote. Harold took to collecting foxgloves growing in a nearby wood and transporting them back to the garden in a rickety old pram – an extreme (but impressive) act, even for someone as frugal as him.

They soon sunk into debt so deeply that when their friend Hilda Matheson took over the couple's bookkeeping she scolded them for the figures. The couple's outgoings were double their income, she said. She told them to decrease their spending or increase their work. They decided to do the latter. They organised a book tour of America, scheduled for 1933. They said farewell to their garden, which was settling down for the winter, and departed from England by ship on 29 December 1932. It was the beginning of Vita's Grand Tour. La Dolce Vita.

When they arrived in New York City, Vita and Harold stayed at the Waldorf Astoria, where they met and befriended Charles Lindbergh and Anne Morrow Lindbergh. (The Lindberghs later leased Long Barn from Vita – who did not sell it – in 1936 to avoid the never-ending attention of the American press. Charles Lindbergh later described this period as among the happiest years of his life.) Both New York City and much of America were in the grips of the Great Depression when Vita and Harold arrived in Manhattan, but people still came out to listen to Vita speak. They were curious about this aristocrat who had become a gardener, although the public relations spiel was a little exaggerated. 'She has inherited the biggest house in England,' wrote one newspaper journalist in almost breathless excitement. When they saw headlines like this, Americans were of course enthralled. No wonder Vita was feted. Harold wrote to the boys, telling them of their mother's new celebrity status. 'Really, it is extraordinary how famous she is,' he relayed, almost incredulous of the crowds.

During this event-packed tour of America, Vita had tea with President Hoover at the White House, and visited Washington, Boston, Ohio, Chicago and Kentucky. She eventually reconnected with Harold (who had left her to get on with it) in Washington on 25 February. From there they travelled to California. In the sunshine of Los Angeles, Gary Cooper showed them around Hollywood, and William Randolph Hearst invited them to stay at his castle, but they declined: they were desperately in need of a rest. After some time to themselves, they travelled to the Grand Canyon on 1 April, where Vita was deeply impressed with the landscape in all its raw magnificence. They then journeyed back to the East Coast again, to Charleston in South Carolina, before travelling by ship home to England. They had visited fifty-three cities and spent sixty-three nights in trains. It was a memorable trip for both of them but, for Vita, it was the experience of a lifetime. She would never forget being feted like that.

After their grand American tour, Vita and Harold were pleased to arrive home to the quiet splendour of Kent in late spring. Their lives felt fulfilled. But it was not to last. Before they embarked on their book tour, Vita had felt confident enough in her horticultural abilities to begin giving talks on gardening on the BBC every Friday evening. (These were later printed in the *Listener*.) She often used Sissinghurst as an example when talking about gardening. Her talks drew more and more listeners. Sissinghurst soon became its own radio star. It is not known what Harold thought of his wife's new fame in England, although he had not minded it in America. It could not have been easy for him seeing her go from one success to another in her career, given that he often struggled with his own career, and rarely had money. (Which is why he tried to be careful with what money he had.) While Vita was no doubt delighted by her success, she was probably feeling a little burned out, too. Book tours are exhausting for all authors. Whether it was for these reasons or other external issues, cracks in the couple's marriage were beginning to show. Vita was certainly beginning to feel some kind of strain. In October she was walking along by the lake when she collapsed. She tried to dismiss it to Harold as 'nerves', but it became worse. Harold later wrote that she began 'sobbing by the lake in the dark', and, understandably, became worried about her 'emotional storms'. Vita, he felt, was 'moving deeply among the shadows'.

On Christmas Eve 1933, there was a terrible scene. The events are slightly confusing, depending on which biographer tells them, but it seems to have involved the family listening to the Christmas broadcast, Vita storming out and the family trooping down the stairs 'with bowed heads'. On the final day of 1933, Harold was deeply worried about his wife. He wrote (in his diary) of her 'nerves' and talked of an approaching 'climacteric': 'I cannot but feel that the next two years will be difficult for her, and unhappy.'

If only they knew what was ahead.

7

Rose Adventures through Sicily and Provence

'I travel in gardens…'

Tom Robbins

While Vita and Harold Nicolson were settling into Sissinghurst, Maud and Leonard Messel continued to embark on botanical expeditions to Europe, searching for rare and old roses. Maud relished these adventures; she always found forgotten roses (among other plants) in the French and Italian countryside, and in the botanical gardens and grand old gardens of their European friends. Many of the pages in Maud's garden diaries from the early 1930s show how many trips Maud and Leonard made to Europe in search of rare and unusual roses and plants.

23 March 1933
Started out for South of France, Italy and Sicily. Sent Comber [Nymans' head gardener] many baskets of bulbs of orchids and plants from the gardens and hills.

5 May 1933
Planted seeds: 1 old pink rose [from] San Domenico Palace Gardens, Taormina, Sicily, Italy (found April 6); 1 wild rose [from] Raffadali, Sicily, Italy (found April 11); 1 old rose, [from] Botanical Garden, Messina, Sicily, Italy (found April 18).

6 May 1933
Planted seeds: Old rose [from] Botanical Garden, Messina, Sicily, Italy; rose, sweet briar; rose [from] experimental garden, San Remo, Italy (two planted).

23 May 1933
Planted roses: rose near Bosco, Italy; rose from woods near Mrs Collins' garden; rose from woods near Asciano, Tuscany; rose near Arezzo, Tuscany, Italy; rose from wood [in] Tuscany.

20 March 1934

Left for Italy. Found rose hips and orchids in the country around Umbria, Italy. Lennie sent 49 boxes back to England and to Kew [Gardens]. All reached their destination safely. [Lennie was perhaps Maud's assistant. She probably sent her roses back to England by train, and had both Lennie and locals to assist with the boxes and shipping.]

22 May 1934

Rose from hedge of orchard near Florence, Italy. Old rose in drive at Asciano, Tuscany, Italy. Wild rose found at Futa Pass near Florence, Italy.

22 March 1935

Left for Italy and Sicily. Lennie collected in the country around Naples. Lennie and Annie collected plants in the hills and country around Sicily. Collected rose hips from the old roses in San Domenico Palace gardens, given to me by the head gardener. Lennie sent back 52 boxes to Comber and to Kew.

❦

By the spring of 1932, Maud Messel's magnificent rose collection at Nymans was significant. *Country Life* magazine asked if it could run a story on it. In the end, it did three. The garden was featured over three issues in September 1932.

By now Maud was a serious plant collector. A serious rosarian.

❦

In his book, *The Road to Le Tholonet – A French Garden Journey,* garden writer and broadcaster Monty Don wrote about the role that gardens play in conveying our aspirations, but he also wrote about the role they play in shaping our character and our spirit. Like Maud Messel, Monty meandered around the back roads of southern Europe, seeking quiet corners and hidden gardens, and the botanical treasures that might be found in them. He looked for the nuances of nature in the landscapes, but he also looked for the histories and stories of the flowers and plants

– the roses, the trees, the topiary and grand Mediterranean scenes. I think Maud Messel did the same. She was as interested in the provenance of old roses, the stories behind them, as she was in saving them. Like Monty Don she had never received formal training as a gardener, and I think that is why she was so eager to travel widely on these horticultural pilgrimages. It was, in a way, her botanical education.

'Our gardens are biographies,' said Hamish Bowles, the renowned writer and editor of the magazine *World of Interiors* in 2022, after he overhauled the publication. Actually, his full quote was: 'Like the clothes we wear, our environments are expressions of who we are. Our rooms and even our gardens are biographies.' Winston Churchill, himself a keen gardener, also believed that our homes and surrounds shape us in surprising ways. I agree. Gardens have made me – and many others – a better person: more patient, more tolerant, more gracious – and certainly more grateful for the natural world. And – just as Maud Messel and Monty Don loved travelling around the world in pursuit of flowers, gardens and landscapes – I continue to seek out gardens in foreign countries. I do it to supplement my horticultural education, but I also do it for the stories and histories that these flowers, gardens and landscapes offer.

On 6 May 2016, I flew to the South of France to shoot a garden for a book. The garden is called 'La Louve', and it was created by the former creative director for Hermès Paris, Nicole de Vésian. It sits in the fashionable village of Bonnieux, high in the hills of Provence in southern France. As I packed for the trip, a few days before the long flight from Australia, I realised that it had been exactly 86 years since Vita and Harold had signed the contract to buy Sissinghurst, on 6 May 1930. I decided to pack Vita's *Country Notes in Wartime* to read on the journey, in tribute to her. I had not yet thought of writing a book about Vita, or roses. I simply loved Vita's writing and I thought it would be fitting to take some of her words to read on the journey. I also recalled how Vita ran away to the South of France on many occasions, with one or another of her loves. By reading her book on my journey, I hoped to understand her a little more. And it was a light book – so it would fit into my carry-on bag!

The flight landed at Nice in the golden light of a Côte d'Azur afternoon. The sky was the colour of an old rose – antique pink. There was a breeze heavy with jasmine and May roses – that quintessential Riviera scent. I hired a small Mercedes the colour of *bleu d'azur* and began the long difficult drive to Bonnieux, using a steering wheel on an unfamiliar side. Several nerve-wracking hours later, I arrived at the village. The light was a lilac-blue hue – *l'heure bleue* at its most beautiful. The scent of May roses was everywhere. The rose scent is more pungent in the late afternoon and evening. I walked around the village, trying to find the garden of La Louve. Wild roses were rampant, poking out from corners of cottages, tumbling over stone walls, and growing wild on the sides of the roads. I finally found the garden and photographed it all before the sun set (the owner had instructed me to arrive then: it was, she said, the best time to shoot it), and then I drove to my hotel, a beguiling hideaway called Le Pavillon de Galon. Pavillon de Galon is an old hunting lodge that overlooks a purple garden, which at that time was floriferous with spring irises. Both it and La Louve are painterly landscapes, designed to reflect the textures, colours and light of Provence, which glow mauve in spring and summer. That evening, I read Vita's book. It was crumpled and covered with dust and smelled faintly of roses after I had tucked some wild roses in the front of it. *Country Notes* is a hymn to the strength of the human spirit during wartime. Published in 1949 by the Hogarth Press, Leonard and Virginia Woolf's publishing house, it is a collection of Vita's columns, 'Country Notes', that appeared in the *New Statesman* in 1938, 1939 and 1940. Each column is delightfully short so it's easy to dip in and out of them before you go to sleep. She describes her life in the country, and her garden, at the onset of the Second World War. She gave the book the subtitle 'Reflections on a Memorable Year in an Unchanging Rural England', and while it seems an incongruity given England *was* changing dramatically at this time, Kent's mellow landscape was a serene respite. Vita, cloistered within Sissinghurst's high brick walls, felt protected. On the first page, she writes of scything grass in August: 'I was alone and the world seemed very gentle.' Her command of language is masterful; she speaks of the silver light on the purple lake at midnight as a 'mysterious lucency'. She acknowledges the 'prospect of devastation hanging over [England]', and admits she sometimes succumbs to despair. 'So deep a grief and sorrow that they are not expressible in words.' She talks about fostering rare plants – 'my wartime evacuees' – for a neighbour in his absence, and delights in their company. She is pleased her pomegranate survives the rigours of winter but worries for her roses – 'I must say it comes as a shock to find how badly the China roses have suffered.' The species roses, she notices, have fared better.

The most poignant column is entitled 'APOLOGIA'. In it, she writes: 'It is not easy to write these notes amidst the anguish and anxiety of Europe. The smother fire of the garden becomes only too readily symbolical, and the destruction of harmless, civilized, cultivated plants equally symbolical. My only excuse can be that the determination to preserve such beauty as remains to us is also a form of courage.'

It is a beautiful, brave, heartbreaking soliloquy. Even though I was reading the words in springtime Provence, decades after the war had ended, I shuddered at the awfulness of what she and so many others had endured. No wonder Vita looked to her roses and her garden for beauty, for reassurance, for a purpose to get out of bed in the morning, even if it was only to care for her plants. She had to keep living, of course, for her husband and for her two sons, who were away at war. But the garden seems to have been her life force, her impetus to continue even during the darkest days. 'My only excuse can be that the determination to preserve such beauty as remains to us is also a form of courage.'

On the way back to Nice the next day, I decided to drive via Grasse and the famous rose fields, many of which are now owned by great French fashion houses such as Chanel and Dior, which use the roses in their perfumes. Pickers were beginning to harvest the crop. Everywhere I looked, there were fields of roses. It was one of the most beautiful sights I have ever seen.

I flew out of Nice with rose-scented memories and Vita's book by my side on the flight.

That was when the idea for this book on old roses began to form.

8

The Pomologist
(the Dreamer at the Centre of it All)

'Now that old roses are back in fashion it is easy to
forget that they came very close to extinction.'

Andrea di Robilant, *Chasing the Rose*

Another rosarian who loved the South of France and who was also establishing himself in the early 1930s was Edward Bunyard. Edward Bunyard is not well known in gardening history, but he is the cornerstone of this whole story.

The details of Edward Bunyard's life are becoming better known. There is one fine biography, published recently, called *The Downright Epicure: Essays on Edward Bunyard*, and it is highly likely that further books will be written. His life is too curious and too interesting to bypass. And he is too important a figure in the horticultural world. Tim Richardson, one of Vita's biographers, called him 'one of the greatest plant connoisseurs'. Another of Vita's biographers, Tony Lord, wrote in *Gardening at Sissinghurst* that 'Edward Bunyard [was] himself perhaps the most significant champion of old roses during an age when they were all but forgotten.' Edward's own book, *Old Garden Roses*, published in 1936, was one of the most influential books on old roses of its day. He was certainly a significant influence on Vita and the roses she bought for Sissinghurst. She called him her first 'Expert' friend, using a capital 'E' in her notes to emphasise his importance in her life and her gardening education.

In the 1930s, when Vita and Harold were establishing the garden at Sissinghurst, Edward Bunyard was modernising one of the most significant nurseries in England: George Bunyard & Co. of Allington, near Maidstone in Kent. The nursery had been in business for 140 years, managed by several generations of clever Bunyard nurserymen, and had a good reputation. Maud Messel was just one client who ordered roses and plants from Bunyard's, as she indicated in her garden notes: *1934 – Ordered roses from Bunyard's Roses at the Rose Show: 6 Königin von Dänemark; 6 Madame Pierre Oger; 6 Belle des Jardins; 3 Madame Plantier.*

However, when Edward took over the management of the nursery from his father, he had neither the inclination nor the mind for corporate life. He adored apples – which are related to roses (both are members of the Rosaceae) – and was a highly regarded pomologist during the 1920s and 1930s, but his imagination was fired by a far more romantic plant – the rose. Over the course of his life, roses – particularly old roses – would become Edward's biggest passion. They would also contribute to his downfall – and, perhaps, his tragic death. But not before he had amassed one of the finest collections of old roses in England.

According to the fine writer and biographer Joan Morgan, one of the knowledgeable pomologists, rosarians and academics who contributed research and writing to *The Downright Epicure* (Edward Wilson, Emeritus Fellow of Worcester College, Oxford, was another), Edward felt that old roses had a romance that modern roses lacked. He also loved their scent, and their associations with history and art. As he later wrote: 'To have … the very rose of which Petrarch or Chaucer wrote, or one which Botticelli or Crivelli painted so lovingly, will to most of us lend an added glow to its beauty.'

Edward became obsessed with old roses, to the point that he began to build up a collection of them at the family's nursery and to propagate them for sale. 'Bunyard's nursery had always sold the plants,' wrote Joan Morgan, 'and as part of its push to appeal to ordinary people rather than competitive rose exhibitors, his nursery's marketing suggested that these were "roses for the mansion, rectory, farm house, villa and suburban garden."'

Although Edward's nursery was not the largest in England it was, according to Joan, arguably the nursery with the most diverse selection of roses, especially of old roses. Its pre-war catalogues list almost 500 varieties. A separate section of the catalogue was devoted to old roses, which increased in number each year until 1939. Edward's personal collection was even greater than the catalogue.

Edward then began supplying roses to other notable gardeners and rose collectors, including Vita Sackville-West, Constance Spry (who was beginning her collection at her garden in Kent), Lawrence Johnston at Hidcote and Heather Muir at Kiftsgate (next door to Hidcote in Gloucestershire). As Joan Morgan wrote in *The Downright Epicure*, Edward's passion fired the enthusiasm of some of the leading gardeners of the time. In turn, Edward's expertise gave him entry into

England's 'high society' of horticulture. '[He was] already mixing with the gardening aristocracy through the RHS,' wrote Joan Morgan. 'Now he would make contact, in his search for roses, with the upper-crust English gardeners.'

Through these horticultural contacts, Edward started to discover many 'lost' roses that were so rare that they were thought to have died out but, in fact, had merely been forgotten and were still growing in corners of gardens, great and small. He took cuttings or budwood of these 'lost roses' and propagated them in his nursery. According to Edward himself, who wrote about them in *Some Rose Memories of 1937*, he also inherited roses from Ellen Willmott's garden after her death in 1934. And he wrote about visiting the Messels at Nymans – Edward knew Leonard from the RHS Library Committee. The Nymans Visitors Book records eleven visits from Edward between July 1928 and June 1939.

As with Maud Messel, Edward's passion for old roses motivated him to travel abroad, to see the great rose gardens of Europe as well as the gardens of friends in France and Italy. Edward had studied in Paris when he was younger – part of his apprenticeship in the nursery trade had been in the French city – and as a result he loved France. He loved its gardens, its formality, its food, its refined living. Paris and the French Riviera were to become his favourite culinary and gardening playgrounds, although he adored Italy, too. He soon became something of a *bon vivant*, as fond of fine wine and food as he was of roses. Slowly these expensive habits wore down his financial capital. In fact, his personal extravagances and inattention to business were probably his undoing. But that sad chapter is to come. Between 1936 and 1939, he was living the best days of his life. It was certainly the peak of his professional career.

In 1936, at the age of 57, Edward published his first book, *Old Garden Roses*. He had plenty of material from his nursery catalogues to use. (Graham Stuart Thomas's *The Old Shrub Roses* also grew out of Hillings' catalogue.) *Old Garden Roses* was published by *Country Life*, the same publisher that had featured Maud Messel's rose garden at Nymans, and is still popular with horticultural customers of second-hand book dealers. Edward wanted to share his knowledge of old roses, and perhaps enhance his reputation on the subject at the same time. It was an immediate hit. As the *Irish Times* put it years later, it was a 'book destined to whet appetites, with a wealth of historical background'. Encouraged, Edward then produced another book – more of a booklet – called *The Manual of Shrub Roses*. His aim, he said in his introduction, was 'bringing forth these lovely things from retirement'. Joan Morgan points out that old roses were a minority taste before Edward published his book. The writer Brent Elliott in his RHS book *The Rose* suggests that *Old Garden Roses* was one of the first books devoted solely to old roses. Brent Elliot is correct. Where Ellen Willmott's famous book was almost completely devoted to species, Edward Bunyard's dealt with Gallicas, Damasks, Bourbons and other old roses. The focus on old roses was completely new – a bold move away from the Hybrid Teas that were then the height of fashion. 'The Hybrid Teas reigned supreme at this time, and old rose aficionados such as Edward were campaigning for the older cultivars, so they did not die out completely,' said Brent Elliott. 'Without the support of people such as Edward and his book(s) on roses, there was a good chance old roses would have been forgotten by the 1940s.' Indeed, Bunyard's books did what he had hoped they would do – they helped both his brand and his business's bottom line. Soon the nursery was selling ever-increasing numbers of old roses.

Vita was just one of the many who bought a copy of *Old Garden Roses* for her library at Sissinghurst. 'Vita's interest in roses was piqued afresh by a book, Edward Bunyard's *Old Garden Roses*,' wrote Tim Richardson in *Sissinghurst: The Dream Garden*. '[Edward's] book on old roses reflected an obsession with near-vanished varieties, which clung on only in the gardens of a few knowledgeable gardeners of romantic disposition in Britain, Northern France and Belgium.' Another biographer, Matthew Dennison, confirms that by 1937 Vita had become a good friend of Edward's, and not just because they lived near to each other's properties. She considered him an expert on old roses and sought him out for his advice. Vita's gardening notebooks, preserved at Sissinghurst, contain many references to Edward, as well as questions to ask 'Mr Bunyard', as doubtless she called him.

In January 1937 Vita invited Edward to Sissinghurst for lunch. Knowing he was an epicure, she led him into a warm room (this itself was a treat: Sissinghurst's rooms were usually freezing) and served him a magnificent feast: woodcock sitting on a bed of *pâté de foie* surrounded by an embroidery of truffles, alongside a fine bottle of Clos de Vougeot 1911 and another of Château d'Yquem, with a cigar to finish the meal. She later described the occasion in a letter to her husband as 'a lovely orgiaical [*sic*] day with Mr Bunyard'. After lunch – when Edward was 'well fed and well dined' – they wandered through the garden, even though it was in its winter dormancy, and talked about roses. Winter is a good time to order roses, because bare-rooted ones can safely be planted any time before spring arrives. Edward had nearly 450 varieties of roses for sale by this time. Vita could never resist a rose catalogue: 'I ordered recklessly!' she confessed.

At the end of their walk through the garden, Vita showed Edward the mysterious rose she had not been able to identify on the first day she saw Sissinghurst. It was a vigorous old rose with magenta-coloured petals. She suspected it was an old Gallica. Edward could not place it – not in winter. Vita later named it 'Sissinghurst Castle'.

Vita's growing friendship with Edward coincided with her burgeoning interest in old roses. Writer and biographer Jane Brown believes that Edward was Vita's main mentor during this period of her gardening life. He was certainly a frequent visitor to Sissinghurst. The author Simon Morley also feels that the two were close at this period. In *By Any Other Name: A Cultural History of the Rose,* Simon writes that Edward not only inspired Vita to introduce more old roses into Sissinghurst's garden but also had enormous influence on the roses she chose. Many of the rarest came from his nursery. It was perhaps fortuitous that the nursery of England's greatest old-rose grower and the garden at Sissinghurst were located so near to each other. It meant that Vita and Edward did not have to travel far to see each other's rose collections – and it probably also meant that she invariably bought more roses than she originally intended.

Among Vita's diaries and notebooks during this period before the war there are records of rose purchases from Edward Bunyard of Maidstone, Graham Stuart Thomas at T. Hilling & Co. (these were probably modern roses, as Hilling only stocked those at this time), Hilda Murrell of Edwin Murrell in Shropshire, and Constance Spry (now a rose grower as well as a society florist), who grew and supplied them from her home. There were no doubt other suppliers, but these four names seem to be Vita's main rose contacts. Thanks to these rosarian friends and experts, Vita was becoming – like Maud – a serious collector of rare old roses.

There was a reason why Vita's collection of roses – and the new plantings in her garden – expanded significantly at this time. In January 1936, her mother, Victoria, had died. The two had always had a fractious relationship but Victoria had still provided for Vita at times in her life when her daughter needed money and now, in her death, she had done so again. Vita was left with £5,000 a year to live on (approximately £300,000 a year in today's money); more than enough to buy all the roses in England. Her books were also successful. After her biography of Joan of Arc was published in June 1936, Vita celebrated by planting quantities of old-fashioned roses. She also purchased a large greenhouse and an orchid house.

Sissinghurst was well on its way to having what biographer and garden writer Anne Scott-James called 'one of the finest collections of old-fashioned roses in the world'.

9

Fields of Dreams

'Do what you please, follow your own star; be original
if you want to be and don't if you don't want to be.
Just be natural and light-hearted and pretty and
simple and overflowing and general and baroque and
bare and austere and stylized and wild and daring
and conservative, and learn and learn and learn.'

Florist and designer Constance Spry

It is surprising how many members of the Rose Set lived close to each other in southern England. Vita and Harold Nicolson were in Kent. So, too, were Edward Bunyard and his nursery, at Allington near Maidstone. Maud Messel and Nymans were not far away, in West Sussex. Even Graham Stuart Thomas was only a short drive away in Surrey. This proximity undoubtedly helped both the friendships and the rose collections develop over the years, as they all swapped cuttings or bought plants from one another, recommended nurseries and horticultural contacts, and meandered through each other's gardens.

Constance Spry had joined this close-knit Rose Set in 1934 when she decided to move from Colney Park to the village of Crockenhill, near Sevenoaks in Kent. Connie had been looking for the perfect country property for some time, and when she and Shav (Harry) found Park Gate House, they felt that it was ideal. It was alarmingly run-down in parts but it had good architectural bones. Most of all, it had land. Constance wanted fields to grow old roses and cut flowers for her booming business, and Park Gate House, with its acres of space, was perfect. A blank canvas. Every gardener's dream.

Park Gate House was ostensibly a fruit farm and, having been run as an agricultural concern, it already had the fertile soil and foundations for a flower and rose nursery. With the assistance of her loyal gardener Walter Trower and two students from Swanley Horticultural College in nearby Hextable, where she would later give lectures, Connie began an ambitious programme of landscaping. Her vision was to turn the grounds around the old house and outbuildings into a beautiful and elaborate ornamental garden of perennials that flowed on to fields of flowers grown for cutting. The cobblestoned yard was turned into lawn, the collection of old fruit trees was thinned out to make more of an ornamental orchard, later embroidered by herbaceous borders, and a wild garden was planned. Other parts of the garden that quickly took shape included banks of lilacs, borders of tulips and irises, a pergola that was soon covered in clematis, and a copse of lime trees, whose flowers and branches Connie loved to use in her arrangements. They also installed two large greenhouses and then set about cultivating the two acres of land to create a grand cutting garden.

At the far end of the orchard, west of the main gardens, Connie proposed a rose garden consisting chiefly of old roses, bordered by a hedge of hawthorn and dog roses to protect it from the fierce wind that blew across the open farmland. Connie realised that approaching this rose garden through the old orchard, especially during blossom season, would be a sublime experience. She also planned a fragrant philadelphus walk for the leafy commute from the rose garden to the nursery. It was here, in the rose garden, among her 'most-favoured darlings', that Connie spent much of her time. Connie's biographer Sue Shephard believes that roses were the plants she loved most and the plants that, above all others, were most closely associated with her name.

Connie had been passionate about roses since her childhood, but it was old roses that became her adult obsession. According to Sue Shephard, Connie called them the 'roses of poetry and song'. They appealed, says Sue, to her deep-seated sense of romance and nostalgia. Connie had visited Sissinghurst and seen the old roses that Vita was growing there. Connie's friend Sidney Bernstein, the London-based entertainment mogul, knew Vita, and it was probably he who introduced the two women. Connie appreciated what Vita and Harold were trying to achieve, although the garden at Sissinghurst was only its early years. But it was when she visited Sutton Courtenay in Oxfordshire, owned by garden designer Norah Lindsay, that Connie felt really inspired. (Vita had also been inspired by Sutton Courtenay and its roses.) The garden at Sutton Courtenay had what Connie called a sense of 'flourishing ease and naturalness', and she noted how the old-fashioned roses grew as freely as they would in the wild, along paths and up hedges. This slightly wild approach to gardening appealed to Connie, who liked to pick wild flowers and rosehips for her floral arrangements. During one of her visits to Sutton Courtenay, she stood under a bower of blooms, inhaling the fragrance, and decided that she, too, would create such a garden. It would be a garden of old roses that looked as if they were growing in the wild.

Connie began her collection by buying roses from specialist growers in England, France, Ireland and Scotland. One of these growers was Graham Stuart Thomas, who was later the manager of Hillings nursery, though not yet a confirmed rosarian. She and Graham soon established a close horticultural friendship. According to Elixabeth Coxhead, who wrote an enthralling biography about Connie, Graham came to realise that Connie knew far more about roses than he did: 'The elaborate French names came rolling off her tongue, with perfect pronunciation, to the astonishment of the nursery workers.' When she invited him to see her garden at Parkgate, he was astounded by both the number of old roses and their condition. In the garden were bushes of a size and magnificence he had rarely seen, and at least half a dozen varieties that few people had ever grown, though they included Vita Sackville-West and Maud Messel.

Connie travelled further and further to find her roses. According to Sue Shephard, Connie regularly travelled around England, exploring gardens, searching for interesting roses and plants, and collecting ideas for her garden and books. These gardens included Wisley in Surrey (the RHS garden), and the country estates of her London clients, many of whom shared an interest in gardening. She always returned home with cuttings or budwood. Her favourite old roses were 'Cardinal de Richelieu', 'Charles de Mills', 'Nuits de Young', 'Tour de Malakoff', 'Madame Isaac Pereire' and others that were not well known at the time.

Just as Vita was doing at nearby Sissinghurst, Connie was creating an extraordinary rose collection. In time, Connie's collection of old roses would rival those at Nymans and Sissinghurst. It was a garden of unique, little-known and rare roses. A garden of forgotten flowers.

The email was brief: *Come on Sunday morning*, it read. *I have to have lunch with a friend, but we will have an hour or so – it should be plenty of time to talk about roses.*

The email was from Isabel Bannerman, one of England's foremost garden designers, who, with her husband Julian Bannerman, has designed many of England's finest gardens, including parts of King Charles's garden at Highgrove. They have also designed remarkable gardens at Seend Manor, Asthall Manor (the childhood home of the Mitfords), Houghton Hall, Hanham Court and Woolbeding, Simon Sainsbury and Stewart Grimshaw's garden. Most of these gardens are festooned with old roses – which have become synonymous with the Bannermans and their garden designs. I wanted to interview Isabel or Julian, but I knew how busy they were. Still, journalists are tenacious, so I wrote a polite letter, asking for an hour of their time. I enclosed a copy of my most recent book. To my surprise I received a kind email in reply. *Come on Sunday*, wrote Isabel. *We can talk about roses.*

When the day arrived, however, I was so nervous that I woke at dawn (4.30 a.m. in England in summer), waited as long as I could, then drove to the village. I was an hour and a half early so I waited in my hire car outside the tiny village church, writing a list of questions for the interview. Which is where Julian Bannerman, driving a tractor down their drive discovered me. 'I am very early,' I apologised. 'Go down the drive, Isabel won't mind,' he said waving in the direction of the manor house. But I was still nervous. So, when Isabel greeted me at the door, I offered an olive branch: 'I am sorry. I'm a little early. May I help in the garden to fill in time?' Which is how I come to be in the Bannermans' country garden on a glorious summer's morning in June. Isabel, dressed in a beautiful pink cotton shirt the colour of an old rose and a tan leather vest that was perfect for working amongst unforgiving thorns, was clearly thrilled that someone was volunteering to help in their garden, and raced to find a trowel. 'You can help me identify roses!' she said.

We started at the top of the drive, next to the pond, and worked our way backwards, digging faded rose tags from deep in the soil or, if no rose tag existed, inspecting the roses from their shape and colour. Isabel, not surprisingly, was adept at this identification game. "Cécile Brunner', she said quickly, as I wrote the names down. 'Russelliana', 'Souvenir du Docteur Jamain' – a lovely, velvety rose, which likes the shade, otherwise it goes a bit brown,' she commented. I made a note. "Gloire Lyonnaise', 'Albéric Barbier' – one of the best ramblers,' she said. I made another note.

We continued to work in the sunshine. As I became more comfortable in Isabel's company, I became more confident and began to ask her questions. It turned out that interviewing a rosarian is best done when you working are in a rose bed. How did she and Julian decide which roses to plant in their own garden? Or indeed in their clients' gardens? 'Well, we don't always agree,' she admitted. 'For instance, I love *Rosa* 'Mutabilis' but Julian doesn't like it as much. The older I get and the more I learn, the fonder I become of certain roses. Such as species roses.'

We continued circling the rose bushes, still digging the ground around them to find and identify their faded name-tags, which had become embedded deep in the soil, or underneath the undergrowth of cow parsley (*Anthriscus sylvestris*). We found tags that indicated 'Rosa de Rescht', 'William Lobb', *Rosa stellata* var. *mirifica* and 'Mrs Anthony Waterer'. These were roses I had never heard of but would know as well as friends before the day was over. Isabel relayed a story of how, the year before, Julian became obsessed with finding a rose called 'The Garland', and eventually found one in Scotland. 'It was Gertrude Jekyll's favourite rose,' she added. It was reassuring to know that even the great Julian Bannerman had become obsessed with hunting down unusual roses in far corners of Great Britain. We continued with our identification, as I wrote the names of roses on hastily drawn maps of the Bannermans' garden. We found a mysterious rose – 'very cuppy,' Isabel said, mystified by it. We deduced that it was a Bourbon, but I wrote a question mark on the garden plan. We continued: 'Queen of Denmark', 'Ferdinand Pichard', 'Madame Hardy', 'Jacques Cartier'. I told her I felt confident the last rose was a 'Jacques Cartier' (which is a 'found' rose with a temporary working name) because it has long been one of my favourite roses. 'It is quite fun finding these!' she said, which cheered me immensely, because until that point I felt I was not being a very good apprentice. We walked around the back, to another enormous rose garden, and continued looking for tags, inspecting roses, and listing them all in my notebook: 'Francesca', 'François Juranville', 'Paul Dauvesse'.

At some stage, I realised that, even though it was 2023, we were – like Vita, Constance and their rosarian friends – still trying to identify, collect and preserve unusual and rare old roses. The thought of it warmed my writer's and gardener's heart.

The following week I returned to Sissinghurst Castle Garden, on a serenely beautiful summer afternoon. I was there to have a private dinner in Vita's walled rose garden – the second dinner at Sissinghurst that summer and a great privilege, I knew – and to meet with the Historic Roses Group, the members of which had organised the event. After we had dined on wonderful food, a few of us followed Sissinghurst's head gardener Troy Scott Smith as he walked around the garden, looking at Vita's roses. Troy and some of the members of our group tried to identify some of the unknown roses in the garden, including a few of the older roses growing over the walls. It was a curious and beautiful evening. I wondered if Vita was with us. She would have been bemused by the sight of us narrowing down the names of her beloved roses. Who would have thought there would still be nameless roses at Sissinghurst?

Then again, as one of the gardeners at the event pointed out, who would have thought that many of Vita's old roses would still be alive, sixty years after her death?

10

Stepping into
the Shadows

'War is the normal occupation of man – war and gardening.'

Sir Winston Churchill

The year 1937 was a busy one for Vita Sackville-West and Edward Bunyard. It seemed to be a year of celebrations in London and all of Britain, a time of joy before the tumult of war – before the sounds of sirens and the constant news of death and destruction would tear the country apart. It was as if the people knew what was marching towards them from across the distant sea, and wanted to have one last memorable party, one last swing around the dance floor, one last great luncheon, one last laugh, one last kiss, one last picnic in a country field or garden, before the world as they knew it came to an end.

In London, the festivities escalated on 12 May when the greatly awaited coronation of George VI took place at Westminster Abbey. People everywhere gathered to celebrate with banners, bunting and tea parties in streets and gardens.

At Sissinghurst, Vita's roses were beginning to bud up beautifully, and it seemed that a magnificent summer of roses was on its way. The 'romantic profusion' of blooms that she had longed for when they purchased Sissinghurst was finally coming to fruition. Harold wrote in a letter to Vita on 8 June 1937: 'Never has Sissinghurst looked more lovely. We have got what we wanted to get – a perfect proportion between the classical and the romantic.'

In late March, as London prepared for the coronation and eagerly awaited spring, Edward Bunyard had put away his gardening outfits, packed his most sophisticated clothes, and boarded the train to his favourite destination, the French Riviera.

The Riviera, which stretched from Cap d'Antibes to Mentone and even across the Italian border to Ventimiglia and Bordighera, was known as the 'Covent Garden of the South'. Roses, carnations, violets and other flowers were transported north by the ton on the Train des Fleurs. English gardeners adored the Côte d'Azur. Everything seemed to grow so much more vigorously there. Especially roses.

Edward had become friendly, through the RHS, with several wealthy English families who had a second home and garden there. He loved being part of this Riviera Garden set; he felt at home among the fine wine and food and the conversations about rare plants. In the article 'Some Rose Memories of 1937' that Edward wrote for *The New Flora and Silva* in January 1938, he mentions that one of the people he stayed with on this trip was Lawrence Johnston of Hidcote, who spent the winter and spring period at Serre de la Madone, near Mentone on the French-Italian border. Roses grew rampant against the walls of Lawrence Johnston's villa and in the terraced gardens below, thanks to the sun and warmth. Edward was in his element. The bedside table in his room even had roses on it – including 'La Follette', a climbing rose with deep pink blooms, which Edward later offered for sale in his nursery. The trip was 'a feast of roses', concludes Joan Morgan.

Edward also visited La Mortola, the Hanburys' garden just beyond the French-Italian border, where the roses, including *Rosa laevigata*, grew to incredible sizes under the Mediterranean sun, clothing the villa's balustrades and walls in lavish fashion. Thomas and Daniel Hanbury had introduced roses to the garden in 1867, buying many from local nurseries such as Huber's in Hyères, the Nabonnand nursery in Golfe-Juan, and Villa Thuret (now the Thuret Botanical Gardens) in Cap d'Antibes. They had also brought in roses from abroad, including several from China, and the Damask rose grown for the perfume industry in the Bulgarian valley of Kazanlik. (Side note: in August 1903, Sir Thomas bought the sixty-acre estate of Wisley in Surrey, whose garden was made by the industrial chemist George Fergusson Wilson, who had died the previous year. Sir Thomas Hanbury gave it to a trust for the benefit of the RHS. It is still the Society's main garden. When Thomas's son, Sir Cecil Hanbury, inherited La Mortola in 1907, he continued his father's work. Sir Cecil was also a trustee of Wisley and La Mortola was well known to visiting botanists and horticulturists.) The year before Edward's visit, in 1936, a rose had been discovered at Mortola – thought to be a seedling of the Himalayan *R. brunonii*, but its provenance is still uncertain – and so Sir Cecil had named it 'La Mortola'. When Edward visited, Sir Cecil gave him a cutting of it, which Edward took back to England where – according to Graham Stuart Thomas – it was introduced first to the Bunyard nursery at Allington and later sold also by Sunningdale Nurseries. David Austin Roses is one of several nurseries that still offer *R. brunonii* 'La Mortola' for sale. Edward's visit in 1937 was a poignant one: not long after he left, in June 1937, Sir Cecil died. His wife, Dorothy, continued caring for the garden until Italy declared war on Britain in June 1940 and returned in December 1946 to repair the extensive war damage and restore the plantings. In 1960 she sold the estate to the Italian government. The garden is now the responsibility of the University of Genoa.

Edward Bunyard was so highly regarded among this expat group on the French Riviera that he soon became a member of what was informally known as 'The Gardening Club', which included the American novelist Edith Wharton, who lived in Paris, Lawrence Johnston and the French Vîcomte Charles de Noailles, who had a famous modernist garden at Hyères and, after 1947, started a new garden just outside Grasse. In his writings, Edward describes motoring from Cap d'Antibes 'en route to the Riviera', dining on the best French asparagus he had ever eaten and taking in the splendour of the roses in his friends' private gardens.

Edward stayed on the French Riviera from late March until early April 1937. He returned to London attend the Chelsea Flower Show with three exhibits – for apples, irises and roses. The roses, which had come from his nursery at Allington, had to be forced to be ready for the show. Edward had transferred the plants to pots the previous winter and sheltered them under glass before the show to bring them to flower. He also exhibited at Chelsea in 1938, when his old roses were awarded the Banksian Medal for the best exhibit at RHS shows during the year. After Chelsea, he took himself off on another rose tour, this time around England. He visited Maud Messel at Nymans, where he praised her collection of rare roses, saying that 'they were some of the most complete collections of species and old-time roses that I know.' Then he visited the gardens of the National Rose Society, as well as Wisley and Kew, before travelling north to Yorkshire.

Vita was constantly inspired by Edward's travels, his extensive knowledge, and particularly by his book *Old Garden Roses* – so much so that she decided to spend a few weeks in the summer of 1937 writing her own flower book, entitled (rather curiously) *Some Flowers*. It was published by Cobden-Sanderson late in 1937. The book, although short, was very engaging – and very Vita in that it was an endearing mix of practical advice and poetic descriptions of plants. *Some Flowers* was not a hit to begin with, but having Vita's name on the cover ensured that sales soon improved. In her foreword, Vita challenged all gardeners to look beyond the usual, the traditional, the ordinary and the plain. Gardening, she explained, was a creative process, and it was important to treat it as art rather than just tossing the same old perennials in, year after year.

Vita loved to see roses growing in a romantic fashion, billowing over her head as she walked through the garden, and she loved it even more when they almost obscured the paths. She liked, as the garden writer Sarah Raven pointed out, the 'embroidered exuberance' of them, as they looped up and over Sissinghurst's walls, or – better still – when they intertwined together. She loved the way old roses grew with abandon and wanted a 'tumble of roses', a rambling garden that was 'romantically treated', with 'rich planting and thick under-planting, laced with climbers, [and] many roses'. To achieve this effect, she preferred to prune them loosely and hated to see her gardeners pruning them too harshly. In fact, one of her gardeners, Jack Vass, who moved to Sissinghurst in 1939, once confessed that the shrub roses were always pruned more heavily than Vita approved when she was not looking. (According to a wonderful blog by Sissinghurst's former assistant head gardener Helen Champion, it was Jack who began the tradition of pruning and tying the roses to long, bent hazel twigs in order to increase flowering and bring the flowers down to an easier level at which to enjoy them. This method is still used today.) Vita felt that old roses flowered better if they were not cut down to the fourth outward-facing bud, as many traditional gardeners did. She believed they should be allowed to flower as a 'wildly blossoming shrub' so they were 'fantastically floriferous'. (Sarah Raven's biography about Sissinghurst has wonderful chapters on Vita's favourite roses, while Tim Richardson's beautiful book shows the planting scheme of the Rose Garden in great detail.)

Vita loved shrub roses and grew many old shrub roses and climbers at Sissinghurst. While other gardeners felt that these old roses were passé, she lauded their attributes. In 1937, she wrote: 'They recall everything that we have ever read in poetry or seen in paintings.' She added: 'They usually smell better than their modern descendants.' Vita loved not just their fascinating histories and romantic names, but also their intricate forms and the way they billowed over garden paths and walls. The modern type of Hybrid Tea rose, she felt, was too stiff and artificial.

Helen Champion says that Vita acknowledged the limitations of old roses, such as Damasks, Gallicas or Centifolias, which flower only once or twice a year in a gloriously riotous mass, but she also argued that nobody expected a daffodil to flower out of season. Vita relished the colours of old roses – the subtle pinks, lilacs, creams and whites – as well as their generous scent, their joyfully chaotic, large-petalled forms and their old-fashioned elegance and beauty, and she felt that their merits far outweighed their faults. Vita would later write of them: 'I know that most of them suffer from the serious drawback of flowering only once during a season, but what incomparable lavishness they give, while they are about it. There is nothing scrimpy or stingy about them. They have a generosity which is as desirable in plants as in people.' Most of all, Vita loved the fact that old roses looked like the antique textiles she had always collected and adored. As she wrote in one of her columns in 1950: 'I could go on forever but always I should come back to the idea of embroidery and of velvet and of the damask with which some of them share their name.'

There was just one problem with Vita's gardening style. Her philosophy of 'cram, cram, cram' meant that her rose beds were exuberant but quickly became overcrowded. And space in the garden by the Priest's House was limited. By 1937, Vita's collection of roses had outgrown their home. She began to eye the kitchen garden, on the other side of the tower, as a new site for her rose garden. The centre of this garden had been planted with a circle of yew hedging by Harold and the couple's son Nigel in 1933 – they called this area the Rondel Garden – and the yews were now maturing in a pleasing way. Two years earlier, in 1935, the architect A. R. Powys had been commissioned to construct another brick wall to enclose this garden, which became known as the Powys Wall. It now offered another potential site to plant roses and shelter Vita's beloved climbers.

Vita and Harold decided to move the rose garden to the much larger old kitchen garden, and Vita made another decision at this time – to have mostly old garden roses in this new Rose Garden. Rose by rose, the old Gallicas, Mosses, Bourbons and other types were transplanted to their new home.

By autumn 1937 it was becoming apparent to many people in England that there was tension in Europe, and a war was on their doorstep. Still, they hoped it would not cross the Channel. It was only after September 1938 that most people realised war with Germany was inevitable. As the chilly autumn evenings settled on the Kent landscape, Vita's secretary Mac, who lived in the gatehouse at Sissinghurst, became closer to her employer. The two women began drinking in the evening – sherry, and too much of it. Vita's handwriting became incoherent, which was bad news for a writer who relied on her longhand. (Harold preferred to use the typewriter; Vita preferred to use brown ink.)

Vita continued to work on the garden even as the weather became colder. She discovered a new pink magnolia, slow growing but magnificent, and wondered whether it was prudent to plant it with the threat of war. Would she still be alive to enjoy it in another year or more? The idea of death did not stop her from nourishing the garden. She wrote: 'A hundred years hence someone will come across it, growing among the ruins of the tower ... and will say: Someone must have once cared for this place.' It is heartbreaking to read such thoughts, to know Vita must have been considering her mortality, and making plans for Sissinghurst's survival, so that her beloved garden would not wither away if she should die at any time.

Vita's determination to make Sissinghurst a glorious garden was clear when she went on a spending spree early in 1938, buying so many plants that boxes began to arrive from all over England. Fortunately, she had three gardeners to assist her by this time – Gordon Farley, George

Hayter and Sidney Neve, as well as a Miss Lee, who worked part-time. Vita began to keep a gardening diary, jotting plants, processes and successes and failures each week. It was perhaps prudent: the editor of the *New Statesman* asked her to contribute to the magazine's 'Country Notes' column on a regular basis, once every two or three weeks – until now, she had been writing for them more intermittently. Vita may have felt that her garden notebook was a necessary accessory but in fact, according to her biographer Jane Brown, she was by now something of an expert gardener, especially when it came to roses.

All the talk of war was so dispiriting that, early in 1938, Vita and Harold decided to open Sissinghurst to the public under the National Gardens Scheme charity. They felt that the garden had matured – Harold had always said it would start to mature seven years after they began planting it, and he was right – and with the war coming perhaps people needed a distraction. So, on 1 May 1938, they opened Sissinghurst to the public for two joyful days. It was Sissinghurst's first official Open Garden, and it was a huge success.

The following year, in 1939, they opened for four days. And in 1940, they opened for six days. The customers put their coins – a shilling each – on a bowl left on a table in the entrance. Vita, for all her shyness and reclusiveness (which would become worse during the war), adored her 'shillingses', as she called her visitors. She wrote about them in the *New Stateman* in 1939, calling them 'mild, gentle men and women … homely souls who will travel fifty miles by bus with a fox-terrier on a lead, who will pore over a label, taking notes in a penny note-book'. They were, she said, the 'true peacemakers'.

Jane Brown believes that Sissinghurst was at its most beautiful in the summer of 1939. Those who visited it then, knowing war was just around the corner, probably felt the same way. There have been many NGS garden days since then, many springs, many summers, many flowering seasons. But those first openings, in May 1938 and 1939, had a poignancy that translated into lasting memories for those who travelled far and wide to visit it. Harold cut paths through the orchard so people could wander freely through the fritillaries and blossom in all shades of pink. There were also tangles of wild roses and drifts of white foxgloves. It must have seemed to many visitors as though Sissinghurst was a kind of Elysian paradise.

By autumn 1938, Vita and Harold were preparing for the war that seemed inevitable. Sissinghurst's fireplace was blocked, sheets of asbestos were screwed on the windows, and valuable antiques such as the Persian pots were moved. Chamberlain returned from Munich with the claim that peace had been brokered, but some people were still dubious.

In February 1939, Vita began her new poem *The Garden*. She told her friend Virginia Woolf it was a sort of 'companion to *The Land*'. Perhaps she knew that a war was coming and wanted to preserve her garden, if not in plants and roses then in words and paragraphs and pages. It was as if she wanted to write her *magnum opus* before the world, as she knew it, ended.

(Side note: *The Garden* is a wonderful piece of writing, and it's important to read to understand Sissinghurst.)

11

War and Roses

'If war has an opposite, gardens might sometimes be it.'

Rebecca Solnit, *Orwell's Roses*

T he year 1939 was heavy with tension. And not just across the garden paths of Sissinghurst but across all of Britain.

Vita, increasingly reclusive, had spent the winter of 1938-39 ensconced in her tower, with only the servants, her gardeners and her secretary Mac for company. In early 1939, she reluctantly gave a luncheon for Virginia Woolf and Freya Stark at Antoine's in London, and then went to dinner at the Savoy Hotel to hear some speeches by notable women, but eschewed a dinner at Buckingham Palace as a guest of King George VI and his wife, Queen Elizabeth. 'I just could not go,' she wrote to Harold. (The young princesses, Princess Elizabeth, later Queen Elizabeth II, and her sister, Princess Margaret, later joined the evacuees heading out of London to safer places in the country. The King and Queen remained in London, in solidarity with those who stayed behind.)

Over the following months, Vita's life became increasingly isolated. Harold spent a lot of time in London for his work. Nigel, Vita's son, was working in the north of England. Mac, although very dear to Vita, was not enough. One day, desperate for company, Vita phoned Virginia Woolf: 'This is Sissinghurst 250 – is that Museum 2621? Is that Virginia? I am making an attempt to get in touch!' Vita said to her old friend, trying to make light of the melancholy in which she was living.

By April 1939, usually her favourite month, the solitude was becoming too much. Vita, perhaps wanting company, agreed to open Sissinghurst to the public again. A date was decided: the first weekend in May. The old roses would not be in bloom, but it would be spring, that most joyous of seasons, and everyone needed a mental break from threats of war and misery. Vita and Harold recognised that people needed to see beauty in the face of gloom, and what better way to do it than to open Sissinghurst for what might be the last time for a very long time? Who knew if they would even survive the next few years? Who knew if the garden would be still there after the German bombers flew through? They just hoped their gentle, garden-loving 'shillingses' would come. They did. They came for the walled garden, the romantic tower, the views of England that they all loved, as if they wanted to remember the green hills before the war covered them with carnage. It was if people knew it would be the last such floriferous summer for many years. Sissinghurst was inundated. More than 800 people filed through the doors. Vita and Harold were there to greet them all. Sissinghurst's reputation had extended so far into Britain that many of the country's best gardeners travelled south to see it.

The writer Anne Scott-James believed the garden had reached perfection by this point in time. Biographer Victoria Glendinning went one step further and suggested Sissinghurst had become Vita's métier, her life's work: 'Vita Sackville-West wrote some good books and some good poems, but her one magnificent act of creation was Sissinghurst.' As Anne Scott-James says: 'The Sissinghurst style was clear for all to see.'

Edward Bunyard, meanwhile, was trying to ignore the terrible headlines on the front pages of London's newspapers and the terrifying news coming out of the BBC and other radio broadcasts by escaping to his favourite country, France. He travelled first to Cap d'Antibes for a few weeks, ostensibly for a holiday but also to do business. While there, he visited several nurseries in a search for old roses. He went to St Tropez, where he found an old Damask rose in the garden of an inn and arranged to send a cutting back to England. He then journeyed north to Paris, to the rose garden at Le Parc de Bagatelle, and the garden of Empress Josephine at Malmaison. According to Jennifer Potter, in her monograph *The Rose*, Edward had always wanted to visit Empress Josephine's famous rose garden at Malmaison. But he was disappointed. Walking its historic paths, he was saddened to see the gardener devoting all his attention to the modern roses, whereas the old roses were pruned to death, crowded, often without labels, and generally struggling against neglect. Edward then visited the Parc de Bagatelle in the west of Paris and the Roseraie de L'Haÿ (now the Roseraie du Val-du-Marne), the renowned collection of old-fashioned roses assembled by Jules Gravereaux, on the southern outskirts of Paris. He was happy to see the latter was still being kept with 'trim neat paths and scrupulously weeded beds'. It pleased him to see that Paris 'had not neglected her noble heritage'.

Edward continued to collect bud-sticks on his travels. Back in England, he decided to enlarge his catalogue with these newly collected varieties and devote more pages to a special section for old roses, called 'Old Garden Roses'. And he continued to collect them. Some came from the United States, where devoted rosarians were also collecting old roses, which they rescued from colonial gardens, great estates and even graveyards, if the collector was brave enough to take a cutting from a rose behind a tombstone. And some came from friends in Europe. The author Andrea di Robilant describes these forgotten roses found in forgotten corners of Italy and France as *rose ritrovate* – rediscovered roses.

Following his French adventure, Edward planned a visit to London. The Royal Horticultural Society, with which he was involved, had asked him to the city for a meeting about fruit varieties. At this time, the RHS was governed by a council of fifteen members, mostly composed of scientists and noted horticulturists, amateur or professional. These included Edward, who chaired the Fruit and Vegetable Committee, Leonard Messel (husband of Maud Messel) and the artist John Nash. The RHS was not as extensive as it is now: it published a monthly journal and yearbooks for special interests like irises, and supported just one experimental garden, at Wisley in Surrey. (The RHS at this time was very much an upmarket society and the garden was open only to members.) However, what the RHS did do during this period was promote gardening, via bulletins on the BBC and contributions from gardeners with a pleasing radio voice and a knowledge of plants. (A few years earlier, in 1931, the BBC had asked the society to recommend gardeners to speak on the radio: one of the names the RHS put forward was Vita.) The RHS asked Edward, in his capacity as a specialist fruit tree grower, to produce a report for the BBC on the importance of growing vegetables that were rich in nutrients, which could help feed and sustain people's energy during the impending war. This report influenced government thinking and eventually led to the Dig for Victory campaign. It was one of his final contributions to gardening and writing. During the summer of 1939, Edward's financial difficulties were such that he took up a paid position as Keeper of the RHS Lindley Library. This meant that he was no longer an amateur gentleman but a paid employee and, as such, according to the rules of the RHS, he had to resign from his role on the RHS committee. Before he resigned, though, he offered a caution to the RHS. The collective focus should not be solely on vegetables, he said. Food was important. But so, too, were flowers.

August 1939 was a solemn month. War was coming. Vita became more and more anti-social. To avoid the heat of the day she took to gardening in the cool of the evening. (At other times of the year, she would garden during the day and write at night. Her daily routine often depended on the season.) One night, she was scything and raking a late cut of grass in the orchard when the harvest moon rose behind the apple trees. She did not normally bother to collect a second cut but this year she felt it important to save every scrap. She relished the time on her own. 'I was alone, and the world seemed very gentle,' she later wrote. Ironically, her roses and flowers looked the best they had ever done. Or perhaps, as Vita gently noted, this was a year when 'one noticed them more keenly than usual.'

On Sunday 3 September 1939, a warm and sunny and otherwise unassuming day, Britain went to war. At 9.00 a.m. Britain gave Germany a deadline of 11.00 a.m. to withdraw its troops from Poland. The morning came and went with no response. So, at 11.15 a.m. Neville Chamberlain announced on the radio that Britain and Germany were at war. Then, shortly after noon, he addressed the House of Commons, when most British people were sitting down to lunch, shocked and silent at the news. He called it 'a sad day for all of us'. That night, at 6 p.m., King George VI addressed the British Empire by radio. 'For the second time in the lives of most of us, we are at war,' he said. 'There may be dark days ahead.'

According to James Lees-Milne, who wrote about it in his biography of Harold, Vita was saddened but not surprised. When Vita heard the news, she walked down the garden path to where Harold was sitting outside South Cottage in the sun and said quietly: 'It has begun.' It was, wrote Harold later, an 'unquiet day' at Sissinghurst.

It was an unquiet day across all of Britain.

Many people went out into their gardens to try to come to terms with what happened, and to make solemn resolutions. Harold wrote in his diary: 'I get up early. It is a perfect day and I bathe in the peace of the lake.' Harold could not believe, as he watched the swans, indifferent to the war, that all the flowers, foliage, animals and birds were behaving as if nothing had happened. It was, he felt, a strange scene.

From that week on, weather forecasts were cancelled. The British government worried that any mention of weather patterns in Britain would aid the enemy. Consequently, gardeners looked to the skies, the cloud formations and the seasons to try to predict what was coming, so they could prepare their gardens. It was not easy. There would be no weather forecasts for the next few years. Charles and Brigid Quest-Ritson believe that people would have learned to cope without a weather forecast. 'Country people in particular learn to read the weather,' explained Brigid. 'They can sense if there's a frost coming. There would have been almanacs and yearly records of forecasts, so if they needed to, they could have looked up records to ascertain what the weather might do.' Still, it would not have been easy to garden without weather forecasts. (Harold Nicolson was fond of using a barograph, which reads and measures atmospheric pressure but does not forecast weather or record temperature. It is still in his study at Sissinghurst.)

Most people were convinced that a German invasion was imminent. False alarms contributed to the collective anxiety. In many places, sirens sounded just after Neville Chamberlain finished speaking to the nation, which unnerved people who were already upset by the news they had just heard.

The following months, between September 1939 and May 1940, became known as the 'Phoney War' because there was little fighting. Nonetheless, businesses and organisations took steps to prepare. The Royal Horticultural Society moved its rarest garden books from the Lindley Library to a safer haven in Aberystwyth in west Wales. When the Blitz began, more garden books, references and archives were moved from London down to RHS Wisley.

Others made their own preparations. Ursula Buchan has written a wonderful, memorable and very poignant book about gardeners during the war called *A Green and Pleasant Land: How England's Gardeners Fought the Second World War*. In it, she writes of one gentleman, the owner of a large garden, who watched his young gardener George go off to war. The gentleman was horrified that his gentle, kind soul who tried not to tread on worms was now being trained to stab men with a bayonet. Another woman, Marjorie Williams, said goodbye to her gardener, Ray, in May 1941. They had spent a few days walking through the garden together, going over what needed to be done – how to maintain the tractor, how to clean the tools. Ray looked sadder and sadder as his departure for the war drew nearer. When at last the day came, the two shook hands and Ray walked down the road in the evening light, turned just once to wave a final goodbye, and was gone, into the darkness of the evening, and the war. When she could no longer see him, Marjorie walked into her empty garage, sat down, and wept. At Horwood House near Buckingham, meanwhile, head gardener Harry Thrower saw his gardening team plummet from nineteen to three. On the final day of 1939, Harry was so heartbroken that his gardeners were going to war, and that both gardeners and gardens would suffer, that he lay down and died himself.

Vita was designated as an ambulance driver. It was the perfect role for her, though she often drove with wild abandon. One day, she received a phone call asking if her Buick would take 'an eight-foot stretcher or only sitting cases and corpses'. Such calls shocked her and made her fearful for the future.

Vita and Harold's sons, Ben and Nigel, both joined the army in 1939, and after working in England in various roles were posted overseas in 1942, within three weeks of each other. Ben went to Cairo with the Intelligence Corps; Nigel went to Tunisia with the Grenadier Guards. Later, both fought in Italy. Harold, however, worked in London throughout the war, first as a MP, then as a junior member of the government for a year and later as Governor of the BBC. Vita, meanwhile, remained at Sissinghurst.

Constance Spry was also anxious. She had been through tough times in her life, but this was different. Always the realist, she began to make radical changes to her life at Park Gate House to enable her, Shav, her loyal gardener Walter Trower and his family, as well as their various horticultural helpers and staff, to get through the war. She bought a horse and cart to use instead of a car, at least for the shorter journeys, as fuel was already being rationed. She installed an incubator so she could breed chickens and have fresh eggs for meals. (People were being urged to keep chickens, pigs and rabbits, and to feed them with food scraps.) Connie and Walter's wife, Gladys, picked as much fruit as they could – it was autumn, the perfect season for this – and then busily preserved them in jars using whatever glassware they could find. Connie's larder was soon full to the rafters. Once the food stores were stocked, Connie began to feel better – or certainly more in control. Later, she would turn to the fields and wild flowers for food, harvesting rosehips, nuts, berries, crab apples, mushrooms and even wild watercress to create wartime dishes.

The September weather of 1939 was sympathetic in its misery. For the first week of September in 1939, Kent International Airport recorded haze every day but, as the month went on, the showers rolled in, and they did not stop. It was as if summer was well and truly over. And no summer would ever be the same again.

Britain's declaration of war brought on a darkness of the soul for Edward Bunyard. When the news of war was announced on 3 September 1939, he sank into a depression. There were several reasons. One of them was the war. Another was money. For years, the epicure and rose collector had been living the high life on low reserves of money. He had regularly travelled to Paris, to Italy, and to Nice on the French Riviera, travelling by the luxurious Train Bleu, which cosseted him in the luxurious style that he had become accustomed to. By the time Edward reached his sixties, however, his lifestyle was becoming grander than his bank account. Furthermore, his trips were taking him away from work at the nursery, where he should perhaps have been going each day to oversee production and keep an eye on income and stock. He was a fine horticulturist but, without an adept manager at the helm of his affairs, his extravagant lifestyle was unsustainable in the long term. It's odd that someone as intelligent as Edward did not realise that he was living beyond his means and try to do something about it. Perhaps he was overwhelmed by the managerial commitments of the business. Perhaps he simply wanted to focus on building up the rose collection, and not on the books. Whatever his reason, his nursery's finances were not great, and he didn't have a plan for the future. Nobody did. The war was coming. Most people could barely think beyond October.

By the time war was announced, Edward was in deep financial trouble. He was fast running out of money. In fact, he was close to insolvency. He was sixty-one, and he realised that the indulgent life he had been leading was about to come crashing down. He owned the nursery, of course, so he had assets, and he also owned a valuable library and his magnificent collection of old roses, all of which could be sold to pay off his debts. But who wanted to buy a collection of old roses? Londoners were preoccupied with other matters. Men and boys were enlisting. Roses were the last thing on their minds.

So, on the morning of 19 October 1939, Edward Bunyard took a taxi to his London club, the Royal Societies Club, at 63 St James's Street, Piccadilly, retreated to a quiet, dark bedroom, took his revolver, pointed at himself, and pulled the trigger.

12

Saving Edward's Old Roses

'The treasure stored by this enlightened man ...'

Graham Stuart Thomas, seeing Edward Bunyard's
enormous collection of old roses after his tragic death

Edward Bunyard's sudden and unexpected death shocked many of his RHS colleagues. William Stearn, assistant librarian at the RHS's Lindley Library, learned about it during an air raid rehearsal when someone passed around a newspaper reporting on it. The headline read: 'The death of noted rosarian E. A. Bunyard.' (Stearn realised he had been speaking to Edward just before he took his life, and that he must have had the gun in his pocket at the time.) Stearn later wrote to a colleague, saying that Edward told him he would deal with library business in the afternoon, but never came back. 'My supposition is that he was a victim of the war,' Stearn wrote. 'There was too little to live for.'

Edward did not die straight away. According to his death certificate, he died of a 'a gunshot wound in head' on the way to St George's Hospital. For a gentleman who had lived his life with such refinement and good taste, a gregarious bon viveur and connoisseur who wrote descriptions of roses that were akin to poetry, it was a terrible, lonely way to go.

To make it worse, the circumstances of Edward's suicide, which was a taboo topic at the time, meant that his colleagues, though in shock, were reluctant to talk much about it. Soon Edward Bunyard's name was forgotten – the newspaper's headlines of war distracted everyone's attention. The writer Ursula Buchan believes that Edward's tragic demise was a great loss to horticulture. 'He exemplified the best, most public-spirited kind of nurserymen, the sort who would have had an important role to play in wartime.'

What happens to gardens when their owners die? This is the question that sometimes haunts gardeners during the quiet contemplative evenings when they're wandering their garden paths. What will happen to their garden when they sell or die? Andrea di Robilant suggests that it is all the more poignant for those who have built up rare collections of plants, especially roses. 'All collectors eventually face the question of what will happen to their roses once they are gone. Some entrust their rare cultivars to other collections; others establish foundations to ensure that their roses survive, or else bequeath their collection to some botanical garden.' In some cases, the gardens are bought by other gardeners, and continue to be loved and cared for and cultivated. In other cases, a succession plan is put in place. Vita Sackville-West's collection of rare and old roses at Sissinghurst Castle estate is now owned by the National Trust. In more tragic circumstances, however, a garden may be destroyed completely. When Empress Josephine died, her great rose collection at Malmaison was quickly lost – a botanical tragedy considering the time and energy that had gone into creating it. And Ellen Willmott's once-wondrous rose garden is now a ruin amid a beautiful park, where gardeners and hikers alike go to soak in the atmosphere and history.

In 1939, there was every chance that Edward Bunyard's collection of rare and old roses would be sold off as individual plants to individual gardeners, or in bulk to nurserymen who wanted stock. But there was also a high chance that many of these roses would be lost to the world. People were distracted by war. Roses were the last thing on many people's minds. And soon the British government would be asking everyone to plant vegetables to help in food production – to 'dig for victory'. Edward's roses faced a dim future.

When Edward's executors attempted to sort out his estate, they found they had a dilemma on their non-nurseryman hands. What were they to do with a nursery of plants, much less four hundred roses? They would have called in expert valuers, of course, and then tried to decide whether to keep the nursery as a going concern or to sell off the land, the buildings and the stock. It was late September or October by then, and most of the roses would have been out of season and not looking their best. To their credit, the executors decided to put all of Edward's stock – both the rose collection and the collection of fruit trees – up for sale. After all, it was England. There were still both rose lovers and fruit lovers around. It has been said that before the auction, they decided to contact the highly respected Hillings nursery, where Graham Stuart Thomas was working. Would they be interested in a first look? Yes, said Mr Hilling. And he sent Graham to Kent to assess the collection. Graham took one look at Edward Bunyard's collection of rare roses and declared it – as he later wrote in his 1979 book *The Old Shrub Roses* – 'a treasure stored by this enlightened man'.

Graham later discussed this and other 'rose auctions' with the garden writer Anne Raver, when she interviewed him for the *New York Times* in 1997. He talked about how, when the war broke out, several of England's great old collections were put up for sale and told her he had been worried about these roses. He said he began acquiring the collections. 'I collected all the best from this country, and the oddments too,' he told her. Anne Raver wrote that as the war dragged on, more and more roses began to find their way to Mr. Thomas, including some from private collectors like Constance Spry.

I asked Charles Quest-Ritson about the sale of Bunyard's roses, and whether Graham Stuart Thomas and Hillings nursery really bought them. What happened to the collection? Charles was dubious. 'It was Brian Mulligan, assistant director at RHS Wisley from 1935 to 1946, who alerted Graham to the impending auction of Edward Bunyard's collection of old roses,' said Charles. 'It is not clear whether Graham bought any of Bunyard's roses at the auction, but the Bunyard auction was followed shortly afterwards by the sale of a big collection of shrub roses assembled by Messrs G. Beckwith & Son of Hoddesdon in Hertfordshire, which T. Hilling & Co. bought in the spring of 1940. This turned out to be rather a job lot – mainly species roses – but included a number of old cultivars, including 'Belle de Crécy' and 'Mme Hardy'.'

Charles explained that the two men – Graham Stuart Thomas and Thomas Hilling – were both cognisant that old roses presented a unique business opportunity. 'Hillings nursery had 300 acres of land, upon which they grew their plants,' explained Charles. 'Hillings had to grow vegetables for the war effort, of course, but they also bought what was called "unscheduled land" a few miles away from Hillings, in Woking, where they were not required to grow vegetables. This is where they planted all their new rose acquisitions.'

Both Hillings and Graham were clearly delighted with the Beckwith collection. But did they decide to purchase Edward's roses, too? Of this, Charles is not certain.

So where did Edward's roses go?

Brigid Quest-Ritson believes that Edward's brother stepped in to manage the nursery, so it was not declared bankrupt, and Edward's precious collection of old roses was withdrawn from auction. But she and Charles are not sure.

Edward's 'lost roses' remain a mystery.

13

The Dark
Days of War

'In a time of plague, as in a time of war, I am
powerless over most things except the cultivation
of my own *jardin*, interior and exterior.'

Gabrielle Carey, *Only Happiness Here:
In Search of Elizabeth von Arnim*

The beginning of 1940 brought deep-seated anxiety to Britain. The winter was extremely cold. But for gardeners there was another issue to contend with: the annihilation of their beloved flower beds and rose borders. The British government, facing a shortage of food supplies and nervous that certain foods would run out, given the danger from German U-boats attacking Britain's merchant vessels, strongly suggested that people cultivate vegetables, or – as the catchy marketing slogan put it – *Dig for Victory*. 'It was a bit of war propaganda,' said Charles Quest Ritson, but it worked. Soon, anyone with a garden, an allotment, a field, a plant nursery or even a tiny plot of land to grow things was encouraged to pull up anything with a petal and replace it with produce. This fell hardest on nurseries whose business was based on ornamental plants.

Suddenly roses and flowers were the enemy.

Over the next few months, many people with a flower or rose garden started digging it up with great reluctance to make way for whatever vegetables and salads they could plant from the seed packets that were circulating. Many gardeners decried this, but reluctantly complied. What else was there to do? And so began the terrible destruction of gardens all over England. If people's spirits were not already battered, they would be by the end of an afternoon in the garden spent pulling out their beloved perennials.

The flattening of flower and rose beds all over England was swift and heartbreaking. As Ursula Buchan wrote in *A Green and Pleasant Land: How England's Gardeners Fought the Second World War*, the garden writer Stephen Cheveley decided, stubbornly, to retain his beloved rose bed because sacrificing his roses to war, he felt, was asking just too much of people. Another gardener, an owner of a great estate, told her staff to continue calling her garden 'The Rose Garden', even though it was now being planted out with veg. To her, it was and would always be 'The Rose Garden'.

(1) The ravishing *Rosa* 'Madame Isaac Pereire' is an old Bourbon that was first introduced in France in 1880. It is a romantic fuchsia rose with up to 55 petals and an intense fragrance. This is just one of the hundreds of rare and old roses that Vita Sackville-West loved which are still grown at Sissinghurst Castle Garden.

Clockwise from top-left: (2) Sissinghurst Castle in June 1930, shortly after Vita and Harold bought the estate. (3) Vita working in the garden. (4) An aerial view of the Rose Garden at Sissinghurst. (5) Vita, Harold, and their sons Ben and Nigel underneath the tower in 1932. Opposite: (6) The Rose Garden today, 94 years later.

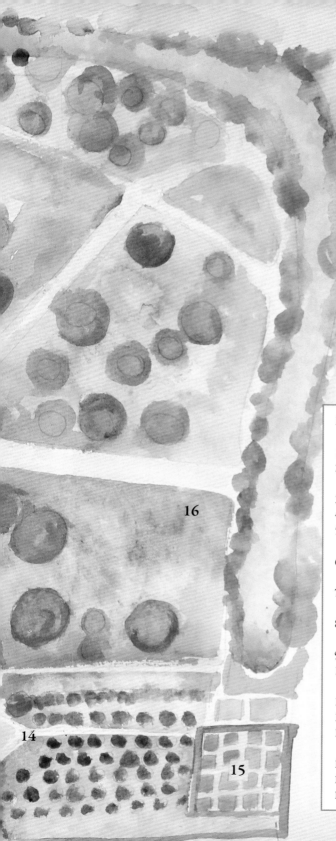

(7) A garden plan of Sissinghurst Castle Garden.

16

14

15

KEY

1. Entrance
2. Accommodation for family and garden staff
3. Library
4. Purple border
5. Tower and Vita's Writing Room
6. White Garden (the original Rose Garden)
7. Priest's House (with the new garden Delos behind)
8. Yew Walk and entrance to Orchard
9. Rose Garden
10. Spring Garden and Lime Walk
11. Cottage Garden
12. Toolshed
13. The South Cottage – Vita and Harold's home
14. Nuttery
15. Herb Garden
16. Orchard and Moat

(8) The Rose Garden at Sissinghurst Castle in June, when the old roses are at their best. Right: (9) The magnificent *Rosa* 'Sissinghurst Castle'.

(10) Sissinghurst's Tower stands high above the landscape of Kent. Inset left: (11) An aerial view of the Rose Garden at Sissinghurst. Inset right: (12) Vita loved pink and purple roses, which still fill the Rose Garden today.

Inset left (13) and Inset right (14) Mottisfont Garden in June. (15) Background: Detail of old roses in the summer rain.

Left: (16) The beautiful *Rosa* 'Constance Spry', which was the first cultivar commercially developed by the British rose breeder David C.H. Austin, and named after the London florist and rose grower. Right (17) Old roses are often distinguished by the number of petals and are usually extravagant in form. They are plants of beauty, glamour, grandeur and grace. Inset Right: (18) The ruins of Nymans are covered in climbing roses in summer, creating a romantic scene.

(19) The grand old walled garden at Stokesay Court in south Shropshire is one of the few gardens in England that has been entrusted to propagate Vita's favourite old roses. The best make their way to Sissinghurst, where they are replanted in Vita's garden. Others are grown and cared for by Victoria and Barney Martin and their team, so they can be saved for future generations. Inset Left: (20) Roses at Stokesay Court.

(21) A selection of old roses.

(A small side story: when the writer Sue Stuart-Smith and her garden designer husband, Tom Stuart-Smith, bought their property at Serge Hill in Hertfordshire, Sue began to fill the beds with old roses. They included 'Belle de Crécy', 'Cardinal de Richelieu', 'Madame Hardy' and 'Fantin-Latour' – 'with its fat petals scrumpled like pale pink tissue paper'. But the ground was not suited to roses, and each season they succumbed to black spot and mildew, until eventually Sue and Tom made the heartbreaking decision to rip out all the roses. To this day, Sue misses those old roses. To this day, the garden – even though it is filled with herbaceous perennials – is called The Rose Garden.)

Vita did not pull out her roses. She chose not to. It may have been that Sissinghurst had land enough for cultivating vegetables, and therefore the need for more soil to harvest crops was not required. (Troy Scott Smith believes this was the case.) It may even have been that Vita, ever the rebellious spirit, simply refused to bow down to the government's anti-rose, anti-flower decree. She may have even thought that the British people had enough to deal with, especially from the madman on the other side of the Channel, and that removing roses from one's garden was a step too far. She was not the only one who thought so. As she wrote: 'The gardening papers have all been urging us not to neglect our flowers in favour of our vegetables ... Man cannot live by potatoes and onions alone! There is much to be said for this argument.'

Whatever the British government ordered, Vita was determined to care for her roses. According to Anne Scott-James, by the time war broke out, the garden at Sissinghurst had been fully planted and Vita was cognisant of the work that had been put into it. She probably wanted to save it, against all odds.

The ironic thing about the war on roses during this period is that while gardeners were being told to pull out their plants to make way for wartime vegetables, children were being told to look for rose hips growing in the wild so they could be used for the production of vitamin C. With imported fruit such as citrus becoming increasingly hard to come by, Britain's Ministry of Health felt that rose hip syrup would be a healthy alternative and encouraged everyone to look for rose hips in the countryside. Children relished the opportunity to collect them from the sides of roads and hedgerows, and in 1941 alone two hundred tonnes of hips, equivalent to 134 million rose hips, were collected and processed into a National Rose Hip Syrup, which was available at chemists for families to purchase.

A handful of nurseries and growers specialised in roses at this time. When the order later came, in 1941, to make land available for vegetables, these nurserymen and women faced the destruction of years of their work. One nurseryman, the great rosarian Harry Wheatcroft, put his plough through a field of 100,000 roses and later admitted it was 'a heartbreaking job'. He estimated that the destruction of his roses had cost him £100,000 of lost stock.

Connie was so upset about the possible destruction of her beloved roses that she drove to Swanley Agricultural College (where she was an occasional lecturer, and knew staff and students well), and shed a tear with her friend Kate Barrett, who worked there. Connie also posed the question many gardeners were asking: *Would gardens, flowers and beauty ever be wanted again?* Kate believed they would and so Connie, fortified by her strength, returned to Park Gate House and decided not to obliterate every last rose and perennial in her garden. In a show of rebellion, she let her roses stay, and instead found other beds to grow war vegetables. She and her gardener Walter Trower then took cuttings of her precious and rare old roses and hid them in a distant corner of the garden, in case a German bomb landed on the estate. Then she drove to London and reassured her staff that 'it was business as usual'. They were happy to hear it but, before long, many of them felt compelled to resign and join the war effort. Watching her staff walk out the door, one by one, Connie began to feel nervous that she would have to shut down the business. She had already closed one of her companies, The Modern School of Flower Work. But then life levelled out again. During this period dubbed the 'Phoney War', people grew tired of waiting for the fighting and resumed their parties, their activities, their weddings and their get-togethers. Many of Connie's wealthy clients wanted flowers just to keep up their spirits. The Covent Garden Market and other flower markets stayed open, and Connie's business continued, albeit not with the same number of staff – or flowers. But she felt that, as long as her clients kept buying blooms, she would keep her doors open to cater for them. Later in the war, many of her clients were American soldiers hoping to charm English nurses and other pretty women in London.

In spring, Connie had a small victory when her third book, *Garden Notebook*, was published. It featured enticing photographs of flowers interspersed with images of Connie's home, with its chic white bedroom, flagstone floors, French armoires and planters, captioned with seductive descriptions of her life and gardening in the countryside. *Gardening Illustrated* magazine was just one publication that gave it a glowing review. Connie dedicated it to Harry (Shav), whose mistress had left to work for the Red Cross in France. For the next few years, while war was raging, Connie's common-law marriage would – ironically – be a happy one.

Over at Sissinghurst, Vita had hired Jack Vass in 1939, a diligent, hard-working gardener who had worked at the great garden at Cliveden. Like Connie, Vita and Vass decided to ignore the war and focus on plans for enlarging and improving the garden at Sissinghurst. In February 1940, Vita placed an enormous order for 12,000 Dutch bulbs, which Jack duly planted (no doubt with help from under-gardeners). Vita was clearly determined to have flowers, even in the face of an unofficial no-flower order from the government. She was determined to 'preserve beauty'. It was, in a way, its own form of courage.

Jack Vass volunteered for the RAF in 1941. Some of his last words to Vita were: 'Look after the hedges. We can get the rest back later.' Vita prayed he would return from the war. She knew she and Harold could not maintain Sissinghurst without him. (Jack did return, but left in 1957 after an argument about the Sissinghurst Flower Show.)

Vita continued writing her columns and articles, which were later published as *Country Notes in Wartime*, even though she acknowledged: 'it is not easy to write amidst the anguish and anxiety.' At times during the war years, the beauty of Sissinghurst's garden, and indeed of gardens all over Britain, seemed almost 'unendurable', according to Vita. 'Nature is mocking us,' she wrote. At other times, Vita felt that nature was trying to console her.

By April 1940, Vita was still melancholy. 'Nature seemed to have gone Nazi,' she wrote. Her humour was still intact, even if her spirit was fading. Vita's bleak outlook remained for some time. 'For most of us the early hours are the worst. [It is] when the nightmare slowly turns out to be not a nightmare at all but the far more terrible truth, when the loneliness of the soul overcomes us.' It was during the still of the mornings in spring 1940 that Vita really noticed, and shuddered at the 'thrum of engines overhead'. A two-year-old neighbour called them 'Germits'.

Late spring turned to early summer, almost without anyone noticing. The days came and went quietly, in a series of what Vita called 'frail breezes' – with frailer spirits to match.

The summer of 1940 was, cruelly, a beautiful season, with fine, dry weather and 'fantastically floriferous' roses, as Vita called them. She wrote of a 'softness about the air, a scent of musk and hay, a scent borne from the great white lilies and the tumbling roses'. The botanical reverie was often broken by the wail of sirens across the fields and occasional gunfire. But for Vita, it was a season to remember. The poignancy alone would have imprinted itself on her poetic spirit. It seemed, as Jane Brown wrote, that England was 'suspended in time, during the heat haze of that glorious summer of 1940'.

Vita tried to write, ensconced in her tower, but the stomp-stomp of heavy boots as the Home Guard watchmen walked up to the parapet each night with their rifles slung across their backs, passing her door as she sat in her study, wore her down. Slowly, however, she began to be grateful for their presence, for their company. They were all just trying to do their part and probably feeling as terrified as everyone else.

A German invasion of England was on the cards. It was just a matter of time. Sissinghurst stood directly on the path of the enemy. Admiral Raeder had persuaded Hitler to confine the proposed invasion to the coast between Folkestone and Bognor Regis, but this meant that the Battle of Britain would be fought right over the skies of Vita's tower. It was clear that Britain was in for a tough fight. Vita, normally stoical, began to experience great anxiety. She feared for the bombers overhead. She feared for the poisonous gas, talk of which terrified them all. But, most of all, she feared the dark. The darkness of the situation. The darkness of the blackouts. And the darkness of her spirit. Sometimes she could not distinguish which was blacker. She wrote: 'Every night I go my rounds, like some night-watchman, to see that the black-out is complete. It is. Not a chink reveals the life going on beneath these roofs ... I wander round, and towards midnight discover that the only black-out I notice is the black-out of my soul.' No one realised she wandered the garden paths alone at night. For the most part, Vita was on her own.

Harold tried to prepare Vita for the worst. He gave instructions on what to do if the Germans came to Sissinghurst. Vita should prepare the Buick with a full fuel tank, pack food for 24 hours and then hide her jewels and his diaries in the back seat. Vita had to find Gwen (Harold's sister, who was living in a nearby cottage), the Coppers (their chauffeur and his family) and head for Harold's brother's house in a more remote corner of England, 'avoiding the main roads'. (It is not known what plans were made for the gardeners – undoubtedly Harold had a strategy for them, too. Or perhaps they had decided to forge their own escape strategy.) Vita argued that she could not leave – she was the local ambulance driver, after all – so Harold gave her a Plan B. If the Germans came to Sissinghurst she was to have a bodkin ready (a method of suicide), so she could 'take quietus'. *Quietus.* Was there ever such a gentler word for surrender? Only aesthetes such as Harold Nicolson and Vita Sackville-West could describe eternal rest in such a poetic manner.

Despite her reluctance to leave if German troops were suddenly to wrench open Sissinghurst's gates and brutally occupy the estate, Vita decided to pack a few essentials. She made a list in the back of her 1940 diary. This is what it included: boots; breeches; bicarbonate; *Roget's* (a thesaurus); bodkin, and gloves. There were clothes, too, of course, and her current manuscript and unpublished poems. A cheque book, too. She must have felt such pain at distilling her life down in this way. There was nothing from the garden. No remnants – no cuttings of favourite flowers; no old roses pressed into a beloved book. Vita knew she would have to leave it all behind. The garden. The flowers. The tower. Her beloved old roses. Everything. The thought of it no doubt broke her heart.

Both Harold and Vita believed that Britain would lose the war. Many people did. It was difficult to see how Britain could win. Harold suspected he was on a German hit list, due to his vocal opposition of the Munich settlement. The couple were deeply worried. Harold wrote in his diary: 'Viti [his pet name for Vita], who is so wise and calm, asks the unspoken question which is in all our minds: How can we possibly win?'

At Nymans, Maud Messel and her family opened their home to evacuees who were fleeing the dangers of London. Maud became 'Commandant Messel', one of the main leaders of Balcombe Military Hospital in West Sussex, which was close to Nymans. There she cared for more than 600 patients during the war. Maud ran her unit like she ran her garden: a tight operation. (Nymans House provided nursing accommodation to house the nurses.)

The summer of 1940 moved slowly across the Kent landscape. It was a warm one, which brought superb weather that lasted well into October, according to records. While the heat was welcomed by the English people, the long hot days gave little reprieve – to plant or person. Gardeners everywhere worried for their gardens. Some spoke of a drought. Vita was asked to judge a cluster of pretty cottage gardens, but the flowers had all died. The owners were apologetic. Vita smiled sympathetically, and quietly assured them it did not matter.

June and July came. Vita's old roses, which loved the heat, erupted into bloom. It must have felt like a momentary pause from the war, a beautiful, blissful, all-too-brief rose-filled season of scent and petal and peace amidst the madness of the year. It was as if the roses were shielding her from the horror beyond Sissinghurst's walls.

Connie was also smitten by her roses in the summer of 1940. Like many other rosarians she had chosen to leave her old roses intact, reserving other parts of her fields and garden for vegetables, no doubt reasoning that there was space for everything. But then she fretted. Nothing seemed safe in 1940. Not even her secret roses that had been spared from the secateurs. So, without telling anyone, Connie arranged for her gardener Walter Trower to take more cuttings of the more precious old roses, which he duly did. (He had already done this, but Connie clearly felt there were not enough.) He then hastily dug a trench against a north wall, out of the way and probably out of the eyesight of any nosy visitors who might betray Connie. He filled the trenches with healthy soil and sand, and planted the cuttings of the rare roses, where they could be left in peace – safely hidden from the world.

Connie hoped it would be enough. She did not realise there was another brutal winter ahead of them – the winter of Mother Nature – and the winter of Hitler.

In August 1940 the government warned that a German invasion of southern Britain was imminent. The warning sirens began. Vita wrote of having 'one's breakfast in peace' before the banshee of the sirens tore through the day's thoughts. The sirens heralded the planes, which flew overhead like a skein of geese before tumbling around each other, gaggle upon gaggle, in a deadly fight among the summer clouds. Machine guns often joined in from below. Wave after wave of German fighters and bombers headed to London. The Kent countryside became littered with the debris of fighter aircraft from both sides.

On one day, Sissinghurst's gardeners counted forty bombers and fighters roaring past. Vita kept tending to the roses. The simple act kept the clouds of melancholy at bay. As the garden designer Isabel Bannerman once wrote: '[Gardening] offers tiny victories, which bolster the soul and help one deal with all manner of setbacks.'

This period was to be one of the most critical periods of the war. According to the BBC, much of the Battle of Britain, as it became known, was fought in the skies above Kent's orchards, fields and villages, as the British tried to repel Hitler's pilots. Harold Nicolson's diary entry for 2 September 1940 read: 'A tremendous raid in the morning and the whole upper air buzzes and zooms with the noise of aeroplanes. There are many fights over our sunlit fields.'

The British people's stoicism, strength and fortitude, not just during the Second World War but throughout history, are famous. There is something in their DNA that makes them as tough as a garden spade.

They may appear to be quiet and gentle souls at times, people of humility and grace and good humour, but when their backs are against the wall, they are formidable opponents. They do not go down easily. This was the case during 1940. When Germany launched their months-long bombing campaigns over London and other British cities, people dug their heels in and refused to concede defeat. Even Queen Elizabeth publicly refused to leave London during the Blitz, or indeed to send her children to Canada when she was strongly advised by the Cabinet to do so. She told them: 'The children won't go without me. I won't leave the King. And the King will *never* leave!'

The Battle of Britain lasted through the summer and autumn of 1940, from 10 July until 31 October. By early September, however, came the news that the heroic efforts of Britain's pilots seemed to be working. And then, at last, came the announcement they never dared to hope for: Hitler had decided to postpone the invasion 'until further notice'. Churchill said of this period: 'If the British Empire and its Commonwealth last for a thousand years, men will still say: "This was their finest hour"'.

The fighting had left its mark, in more ways than one. The blood-streaked parts of the aircrafts' wreckage had stained the soft fields and gentle flower borders of Kent's farmers and gardeners. There were broken shards of planes strewn across the undulating green landscape. It was unfathomable that there was such horror in this, one of the gentlest, most pleasant places on Earth.

Everyone was battle-weary. Even though there was a lull in fighting, the constant talk of war was dispiriting. The Nicolsons had 'bomb-proofed' Sissinghurst, but the idea that the garden they had created could be destroyed at any moment was almost more than they could bear.

Leonard Woolf, Virginia Woolf's husband and Vita's publisher, was similarly grieved by the fact that war had overtaken their lives so that even gardening – that peaceful, pleasant, non-violent British pastime – was being ruined by the ruthlessness of Hitler and his shrieking planes. One day Leonard shouted at the radio that he was planting irises, which would still be 'flowering long after [Hitler] is dead!'

Vita was still drinking too much. The bottles of alcohol helped her sleep through the noise of the bombs falling near Sissinghurst, night after night. In one attack, an explosion brought down plaster in Vita's bedroom ceiling. The experience shook her. She realised that Sissinghurst was not impregnable. As Victoria Glendinning has pointed out, her letters from this time were scrawled in spidery writing, as if written when blurred by drink – or tears.

In October 1940, Vita's dear friend Hilda Matheson, the former Director of Talks at the BBC, died from Grave's disease. She was just fifty-two. Hilda had been with Vita when she first moved into Sissinghurst. In 1930, she had worked alongside Vita in the garden in those first months of settling in. How long ago must that have seemed to Vita. Hilda's death was also hard on Dorothy Wellesley. Vita went straight to Dorothy and found her drunk and incoherent. The same day, Vita learned that Knole had been damaged by a bomb. It must have felt as if her world was fast exploding.

Winter arrived in a thick blanket of mizzle and misery that settled on the landscape, covering England in melancholy. The chill that followed gave everyone the jitters, as if they were not already shaken enough by what they had endured. The blinding white snow fell in blinding white blizzards and refused to leave. Pipes froze, cars were stuck in snowdrifts, railways were blocked, food in larders everywhere froze and even the Thames iced over. Shops emptied of vegetables, as people tried to stock their larders. In January 1941, the government made the tough decision to introduce food rationing.

By February 1941, both winter and war had well and truly settled in. Vita, like many, was deeply depressed. Her dear friend Virginia Woolf had fallen into an even deeper hole of despair. The following month, on 28 March 1941, having endured years of debilitating depression, Virginia Woolf tugged on her garden boots, walked out of her garden gate tucked behind her beautiful home at Rodmell near Lewes, and stepped into the freezing River Ouse, the pockets of her garden coat full of hard grey stones to weigh her down, so that she would sink blissfully into the current. Her body was not found until three weeks later, on 18 April.

When Harold heard the terrible news, he left work immediately and took the first train to Sissinghurst to be with Vita. She was so grief-stricken about Virginia's death that she could not talk about it for a week.

Leonard Woolf believed the strain of the war was the final straw for his beautiful, tender, gentle, frail wife. Vita's son Nigel later wrote in his *Portrait of a Marriage* that 'Virginia [Woolf] was the most remarkable human being I have ever known.' He describes her with such fondness – how she was the children's fairy godmother, floating in and out of their lives with kindness – that it made her death even more tragic.

When Jack Vass left, Vita had one frail gardener and a Land Girl to work with her in the garden. (Later, several more Land Girls came to help.) She came to rely on her dear donkey, Abdul, to do the hard labour. In one letter to Harold, Vita wrote of the donkey's endearing spirit: 'He is so serious and pulls so hard. I gave him a carrot, but he was too preoccupied to eat it.'

Sissinghurst, of course, was not alone in losing its garden staff. All over Great Britain, any employer with staff of an age that made them eligible for the call-up soon lost their workers. Gardeners were among the many who put down their tools, picked up their courage and enlisted – or were called up. There are many heartbreaking stories of how many of these gardeners did not return from the front. And for those who survived and returned, hoping to step back into their old jobs, they had another shock. Their jobs were gone. According to Charles Quest-Ritson, many English employers could not afford to re-engage the survivors in 1945 because taxation during the war had been so punitive – the highest rate of income tax was 99.25% – and many people did not have enough income left to keep house or garden in good repair, let alone hire people to manage their garden.

Inevitably, Sissinghurst's garden grew rampant, until Vita could no longer control it. The grass grew knee-high, although she did her best to scythe it. The beds became full of brambles and thistles and ground elder. The moat was choked by reeds, the flower beds filled with weeds. The Nuttery became a tangle of plants. She simply focused on the roses – the hedges and the roses. At times, Vita felt as though she was fighting two wars: one against the Germans and one against the weeds. She later wrote in *House & Garden* magazine in 1950: 'The rest of the garden just went wild during the war years. We had begun to get it tidy, and then it reverted to the wildness in which we had found it in 1930. We could not cope with it at all.'

In time, the Herb Garden became unrecognisable, hidden by overgrowth. Later, the flowers were trampled by army troops. The sight of it often brought Vita to tears.

Everybody was waiting for spring. Spring is always a sign of better days ahead, but this spring seemed especially poignant. People were anxious. Flowers and roses calmed them, gave them hope. In his book *The Old Shrub Roses*, Graham described how people seemed to long for the arrival of the spring in 1941. When spring did come, and then the beginning of summer, the roses in Vita's garden and Connie's garden, and in those gardens where they had been allowed to survive and quietly thrive, bloomed as if there were no tomorrow. They bloomed as if they knew they had to keep their melancholy masters and mistresses happy. They bloomed as if they knew they had to survive the war.

The gardeners of Britain continued to garden. Gardening is a therapeutic activity, and many found it comforting. But it also allowed them to forget time for a moment, while grounding themselves in the reassuring passage of seasons. The spring blossoms. The summer fruit. The autumn produce. No matter what was happening in the world, Mother Nature remained a constant and calming presence.

When Connie received an invitation from the Ministry of Information to do a series of lectures around the country 'to lift people's spirits', she agreed, but instead of talking about dull subjects such as keeping pigs and planting packets of seeds, she decided to talk about roses. As Sue Shephard wrote in her fascinating biography *The Surprising Life of Constance Spry*, Connie had always been as interested in the healing power of flowers and gardening as she was in the practical aspects of horticulture. According to Sue, Connie had already written of how, during the First World War, people had found solace and comfort in gardening. 'Growing flowers and working among plants and earth [brings with them] a potent and unnameable satisfaction.'

Connie knew flowers were going to be important to get through the war. 'Whatever comes, however much destruction and devastation may be ahead of us, I am quite certain that gardens and gardening and flowers and their decoration will not decline in interest for us, but will become more and more a refuge.'

A woman at one of Connie's Ministry of Information talks wrote to her twenty years later to thank her for her 'flower speeches'. 'You spoke of old roses in old gardens and held us spellbound, and at the end thanked us for listening to you. Nineteen years and three sons later, we have our own roses. I would like you to know how long your words stayed with me.' Connie was deeply moved by the note, and by the effect her simple words had clearly had on an audience of gardeners that was depressed by both the war and the absence of flowers and roses within it.

Connie kept her own spirits elevated with embroidery, which she learned from Maud Messel's daughter Alice. Maud was herself a talented embroiderer and had taught her daughters. Now, Connie was addicted, too. She took her embroidery on her long train journeys around England, whenever she was called to give a talk. She liked to do floral designs, based on flowers from her garden. In her usual sociable fashion she got her friends to do embroidery, too. They, too, carried their embroidery around in their gas mask cases.

In September 1941, Vita was still struggling with low moods. She tried to keep them from Harold, who was working in London for the Ministry of Information (Churchill had asked him to do so, working under Duff Cooper, although Harold felt that Duff should be working for *him*). Christmas was a dismal affair.

By February 1942, almost a year after Virginia Woolf died, Vita was spending most of her days alone at Sissinghurst, with only her dog Martha by her side. Her secretary Mac had left to look after wounded soldiers abroad. (Vita wrote to her almost every day.) Vita had eschewed her cold writing tower, as coal was almost impossible to come by and she had nobody to carry wood up to the fireplace in her writing room in the tower, and had taken over Mac's old room in the gatehouse block. When

March came, and the nights became longer, she worked in the garden.

The months passed.

Vita's son Nigel once argued that 'recluse' was too strong a description for his mother. He felt she was 'solitary'. And it is certainly true that writers need to be reclusive, to get their writing done without interruption. But this period of Vita's life was more solemn than solitary. She faced loneliness on a level she had never experienced. When Gwen, Harold's sister, announced she was moving from her cottage near Sissinghurst to go and live in her husband's house on St Michael's Mount in Cornwall, which he had inherited along with the title of Lord St Levan, Vita was inconsolable. She knew she would be more isolated than ever. She had drifted towards seclusion for so long, having welcomed the antisocial life that a writer requires, but now that she was truly cut off from her family and those she loved, she was deeply worried.

Kent's towns and villages continued to be bombed. Casualties on the ground were often heavy, despite the fact that thousands of people had underground shelters to avoid the raids. On the first day of June 1942, Canterbury suffered a particularly heavy attack as high explosives and incendiary bombs were dropped on the city for more than an hour and a half. Hundreds of historic buildings were destroyed. Entire streets were flattened – or burned. Ramsgate, Folkestone and Dover were under almost constant attack, as the Germans tried to control the Channel. Such was the intensity of fighting around Britain's frontline coastal towns that Kent became known as 'Hellfire Corner'.

Yet there were bright moments. Harold came down from London most weekends. Together, the two of them breakfasted in the garden and often bathed in the lake. These small moments of normality kept Vita's spirits elevated until the following weekend, when Harold joined her again. When Harold went back to London, Vita always packed a posy of flowers and roses for him to take: his own small piece of Sissinghurst. She used a basket, which he took with him on the train. Both relished this small, sweet, weekly ritual. 'I love it when you go off with the basket spilling its récolte,' she wrote. 'I love you having bits of Sissinghurst to take with you.' Some of the bouquets included violets, roses of course, prunus when it was flowering, irises (even though they do not travel well, nor last long in water) and honeysuckle. Harold would put aspirin in the water when he arrived in London, and sometimes the flowers would last all week long.

Vita turned fifty-one in March 1943. She felt old. Most people did during the war. It aged everyone. But she also knew that April was on its way, and spring, for gardeners, is a season of renewed hope. In her poem *The Garden*, there are two poignant lines: *I will believe in April while I live. I will believe in Spring.* Vita was waiting for her favourite month to appear.

(Side note: Vita may have liked April because it heralded spring, and the emergence of her garden, or she may have felt sentimental about the month because it was when she found Sissinghurst.)

When spring finally arrived, Vita found she had unexpected bursts of energy. In the absence of staff at Sissinghurst – or certainly staff to help with housework – she began doing a lot of the housekeeping herself, for the first time in her life. In one letter to Harold she wrote about polishing, which she did for an hour before breakfast each morning, surprising even herself. In April 1943, eager for a break from polishing and perhaps monotony, she accepted an invitation from Osbert and Edith Sitwell to read some of her work at an event attended by the Queen and the young princesses in Bond Street, London. Before the event, Vita visited Sibyl Colefax, with whom she had lunch, then they picked up Dottie Wellesley who was also doing a reading of her work at the event. When it was Vita's turn to read to the audience, the Queen waited expectantly for her to speak. The princesses did, too. The entire audience wondered what she would say. Vita began, with a quavering voice, to recite part of her poem *The Land*. She managed to get through the first part without a fault, but when it came to the paragraph about the moonlight – *that moon, that star* – her voice broke. The emotion of the last few years, of walking around her garden alone at night, under the constant threat of German bombers, came tumbling to the surface. Always courageous, Vita pushed through, but her voice was clearly weak. When she finished, the crowd burst into applause. Even the Queen clapped her gloved hands. Duff Cooper later sent her a kind note: 'You were so much the best – in voice and verse and beauty.' Vita was deeply moved.

Vita had always been interested in history, and myths and mysticism. And so, in 1943, she decided to write a biography of two saints,

Teresa of Avila and Thérèse of Lisieux. Over the next six months, she wrote like a demon, and when she had finished she called the novel *The Eagle and the Dove*. Vita was a spiritual person, as many gardeners are, and this book seems to have been something she needed to write at this time of her life. She may or may not have believed in God (or any deity), but she was still a mystical soul. She knew the subject matter was more esoteric than she usually attempted, but she also knew that people were contemplating such things – life, death and everything in-between – during these emotionally turbulent years. Death, especially, was on everyone's minds. Vita decided to publish it through Michael Joseph, who released the book in early November 1943. The following year they decided to do their fourth reprint so clearly the subject matter was not that peripheral, after all. People wanted to escape reality, and losing themselves in words was one way of doing it. Possibly, those same people felt they could be saved by words, too. What better than a biography about saints to do it?

Vita continued to write during the day and work in the garden by moonlight, often until midnight. Harold wrote to the boys, concerned for her: 'Mummy works too hard … She is dreadfully thin.' Later, it was found that her spurts of energy were due to Benzedrine, a stimulant. The doctor had prescribed it for Harold, and Vita told him how much 'fun' it was to be on. She certainly would have been energised, and it is no wonder she gardened until midnight. Then again, Vita's favourite time of day had always been between twilight and moonlight – *l'heure bleue*: the blue hour.

Meanwhile the war roared on. Harold and Vita continued to trim the hedges, as Vass had ordered her to do, especially the Rondel. Above them, bombers streamed overhead incessantly in huge formations. On 25 July 1943, she heard on the wireless that Mussolini had resigned. Then, on 8 September, came the news that Italy had surrendered. Harold suspected the war would continue until 1945.

There were bright spots in the darkness of it all. Vita's work *The Land* was bringing in royalties, after people began reading it during the war. Vita bought Harold a new suit. He felt gallant.

In October, Vita pulled out her suitcase and drove through damaged East Grinstead to Balcombe House to stay the night with Lady Denman, who was head of the Land Army and its enormous 800,000-strong troop of girls. Lady Denman wanted Vita to write a book about their work; Vita was not so keen. They talked through the project. Vita eventually took it on.

Another quiet Christmas came and went.

On 4 February 1944, Vita's fears were realised when the sirens heralding an imminent air battle began while she was alone in the South Cottage; Harold was in London. As the planes tore through the skies and began their dog fights, Vita watched with horror as the doors rattled with the gunfire. She listened to the sounds of bombs falling so close that she could hear the whistle of them as they seared the air. She waited in bed for the fighting to pass, with her dog Martha on the floor by her side, but she could not stop trembling. Two days later, on 6 February 1944, Sissinghurst's tower came close to being destroyed when a German bomber, crashing in flames, hurtled past, missing it by a few yards. Harold was home at the time, having travelled to Sissinghurst for the weekend. They were both shaken by the near-miss. He wrote to his sons: 'I do not think that Kent is a safe place. I think it is very dangerous indeed.'

(Side note: All mothers worried about their sons and daughters in the war. Vita and Harold's two sons Ben and Nigel, were both fighting overseas. They both survived the war, and returned to Sissinghurst.)

Night after night the bombers streamed overhead on their way to attack London. The garden continued to be splattered with war debris and the fields around filled with parachutes, bombs and occasionally bodies. Vita tried not to listen whenever one of them fell from the sky and thudded on to the fertile Kent soil.

In June 1944, just days after the Allied invasion of Normandy (D-Day), Germany launched the first of almost 1,500 V1 flying bombs, or 'doodlebugs' as they were nicknamed, at Britain. On 7 June 1944, Vita's greenhouses were smashed by debris from the flying bombs, as was a window in her now-abandoned writing tower. The carnage in the garden was such that she had to step around the shards of glass constantly. There was no point in clearing the mess: more bombs would simply fall the following day. As Anne Scott-James wrote: 'Physically,

Sissinghurst was exposed to the heat of World War II. It was in a vulnerable corner of England. When the V1s and V2s started, Kent was first on their hateful path.' Kent had found itself in the front line. It is difficult to fathom now, but this gentle, green, field-and-garden-punctuated pocket of England was now 'Bomb Alley'.

On 1 August 1944, came the news everyone had hoped for: Paris had been liberated. Harold and Vita were overjoyed. They later learned that their sons were in Italy, alive and safe. The couple did not realise it then but they still had a year of fighting to endure before things would improve. At the end of 1944, V2 rockets were fired on Kent, again with devastating consequences. By 1945, troops with tanks moved into Sissinghurst. Vita watched as the army camped in her winter garden and grounds. At the sight of them, her spirits sank into another depression. It must have seemed as though the war would never end.

Jane Brown feels that Vita seemed to reach the depths of her depression in the winter of 1944-5. It had been a long war, and the winters had made it worse. Vita had started writing her poem *The Garden* in the winter of 1939-40, and now, five years later, it remained unfinished. Five years of brutal war. Five years of brutal winters. It must have seemed to Vita, walking around her now-overgrown garden at Sissinghurst, as though gardens would never be the same again. No wonder she found it difficult to write a poem about them.

In early 1945, Vita and Harold finally received some wonderful news. Their son Ben – Captain Nicolson – contacted them to say he was coming home from the war. Vita and Harold had not seen him since October 1942. He had been hit by a truck in Italy, but had survived, and his injuries would heal. Vita was elated. Harold was moved to tears. They would hear from Nigel too before too long

In April 1945, the blackout was finally lifted. And that's when Vita's spirits did too, despite her perennial exhaustion. Sissinghurst had survived. And so had her roses. Her garden was a shadow of its former self and so, too, was she. But she knew that both would recover in time. Unlike thousands of people who would never return from this terrible war, Vita's family had somehow managed to make it through.

Vita turned on the lights in the garden for the first time in five years. The next day she moved back into her tower room.

A month later, in the first week of May 1945, Germany surrendered. After six long years, it was over. People everywhere emerged from their shell-shocked lives, found a bottle of wine or beer and raised a toast to VE Day – for Victory in Europe. Harold and Ben were sitting in the garden when they heard the news. They went to find Vita, who was gardening, and told her. Together, the three climbed the old tower stairs, brushing war dust and debris off the stone steps as they went, and quietly hoisted the family flag. On 17 June, their other son, Nigel – another Captain Nicolson – phoned to say he was in Naples and on his way home. Vita shed a few tears.

Vita's poem *The Garden* was published a year later in 1946. It was reprinted in November and again the following May. It won her the £100 Heinemann Prize. She spent the money on azaleas for the Moat Walk, to make it beautiful after years of doom and gloom. She was also appointed a Companion of Honour in the New Year's Honours of 1948.

While my generation – I am in my early fifties – and the generations after me have not been through a time as terrible as the Second World War, the Covid pandemic was a testing time for everyone in the world, no matter how old you were or where you lived. It required its own kind of courage – fortitude. And for many of us, it was our gardens and our flowers and roses that helped us get through.

Like many people, the endless lockdowns of Covid depleted my spirit. I was already burned out before Covid hit, weary from years of relentless book deadlines and international business travel, from ten years of moving houses and constant renovations. (We moved four times, as real estate was one of the few ways we could make money, mostly from restoring gardens.) When 2020 came, with its negative news on repeat, that was it: I was down for the count. I could barely muster the energy to water my garden, let along write a biography about roses. What I did not realise is that roses would save my depleted spirit.

We live by the coast where the gales are often brutal. One Friday in April, after seeing the news feeds about Covid and feeling a knot of anxiety form in my stomach, a knot I feared would affect everything in my life, from my writing to my future travel plans and even my marriage, I tugged on my old garden boots and ventured outside, looking for serenity and perhaps also therapy in the damp soil. The brutal sea wind was flinging my newly planted old roses around, so their canes looked like a botanical scarecrow. I bent down to mortar the brick borders of my French potager (everyone I knew was putting in potagers, as if we all suddenly lived in a grand manor) with the aged bricks my mother had given us from our former family home. But the wind had other ideas. Sea winds are temperamental like that. They have no mercy – not on old roses, potagers, procrastinating authors, and certainly not on gardens by the sea. I left the bricks and the potager and began to plant the white climbing rose called 'Madame Alfred Carrière'. I knew that Vita Sackville-West had also planted one at Sissinghurst – it was supposedly the first thing she had planted after she bought the estate – and it felt fitting to plant one now on 4 April, exactly ninety years since she had found her now-famous garden on 4 April 1930. It felt like a sign – a sign of hope.

At midday, I retreated from the wind to have lunch and check the news feeds. The bad news was like a terrible drug, a toxin that I needed to ingest. But I felt, as I always did when watching the news, a great melancholy, one that even 'Madame Alfred Carrière' could not lift. Just then our Cavalier King Charles began barking and our Jack Russell sniffed the front door. I raced to find my garden boots and stepped outside, but there was nobody there. Had I imagined it? The sea gale wailed again. The dogs took a lungful of it, and raced around the garden, their energy renewed. I stood and inhaled, too. And then I noticed the rose book in a corner of the veranda, hand-delivered by a dear friend. She had come and gone quietly, like a fairy in the wind. I sat on our front step and opened a random page. My hand fell on to a paragraph about 'Madame Alfred Carrière'.

Suddenly the day felt curious and strange.

The great Renaissance Swiss physician and alchemist Paracelsus, a pioneer of medicine, once described fairies as 'elementals' in the garden, and if I am taking off my journalist's hat and putting my writer's one on, it did indeed feel as though there were sylphs or 'faeries of the air' dancing on the salt spray that day. Paracelsus also believed that sickness and health in the body, whether physical or mental, rely upon the harmony between humans (microcosm) and nature (macrocosm). I, too, believe that now. As Vita and her rosarian friends learned, we sometimes need the earth to ground us in times of terror and pain, to show us the way. I took the delivery of the rose books from my friend and an armful of the last old roses in my garden, which were clinging on in the wind, and I carried them inside and bundled them into a vase. A curious alchemy began working. My emotions, held in check for so long through the weeks of Covid-induced anxiety and worry, gave way. I began crying. And then, prompted by a force I still cannot explain, I put the vase of old roses on my desk, and I began writing.

I stepped into the world of Vita's roses once more.

A month or so later, the same friend who quietly dropped the rose book on my doorstep phoned to tell me she was moving to another state, and that she had decided to gift me all the old roses from her garden. She felt I should adopt them; she thought I would be a wonderful foster mother for her plants. I was terrified but accepted. She gently pruned each one, lifted them all, potted them into large pots with fresh potting mix, and then phoned me to say: it is time; come and collect them. My husband took his truck and when he returned to our house with the back piled high with roses he looked like a rose farmer. I was both elated and alarmed. Where was I going to plant them? The roses looked as nervous as I was. In time, we found room for them all in our garden by the sea.

Then spring arrived. It was one of the wettest springs that many of us here in Melbourne can remember. Rosarians, tender and experienced alike, know the worry that comes with a wet spring, but this was alarming in its ferocity. Parts of the garden flooded, enormous 100-year-old trees collapsed around us from waterlogged roots, and capricious winds blew over a couple of the roses. Despite this, most of the old roses prevailed. They were bedraggled, but they were brave.

On one of these rain-soaked days I ventured into the garden during a break between the showers to check on them. The roses, drooping forlornly, were so waterlogged they looked as if they were weeping. I felt emotional myself. The weather forecast warned of yet more rain ahead for the weekend – up to 100 millimetres – and I prayed to Mother Nature to let the roses live. She could take the beautiful anemones, the bearded irises, even the *Papaver* 'Royal Wedding', a fussy flower which flowered intermittently but was ravishing when it did, but the roses, the old roses, they could not be replaced easily.

I thought of Edward Bunyard, Vita Sackville-West, Constance Spry, Graham Stuart Thomas, Maud Messel and all the other dedicated rosarians, and how they went to enormous lengths to save these magnificent old-fashioned roses during the war and in the years after it, so that we might enjoy them many decades and many floriferous rose seasons later. I whispered to the roses that I would do everything I could to ensure their survival in my own garden. Because I knew that, for a little while, it looked as if there might be very few old roses at all.

14

Blooming Again
After the War

'Garden as though you will live forever.'

Eighteenth-century landscape architect, William Kent

T he years following the war were a period during which people put their lives back together, piece by broken piece. Many did not make it home.

The war had caused great havoc in the gardens of England, especially the grand gardens and estates. After the war, the owners of these large gardens faced difficulties. Many of their head gardeners, their under-gardeners and their garden labourers had died in the sludge of the European front or the deserts of North Africa. Without skilled people to restore and care for these grand gardens, it was difficult to see how they would return to their former glory. In addition, their owners could only afford a fraction of the staff they had employed in 1939, before the war.

At Nymans, Maud and Leonard Messel had lost many of their gardeners to the war. 'There were twelve or so gardeners before the war, but very few after the war,' explained Caroline Ikin, Nymans' curator. The war had a disastrous effect on both the family and the estate. 'Three of Leonard and Maud's nephews were killed in action, and the garden suffered from a lack of attention due to the severe reduction in staff.'

The Messels were contemplating how to move forward when another tragedy struck. At the beginning of 1947, on a snowy, winter's night in February, Nymans caught fire.

Leonard's diary entry for 18 February, 1947 read:

'Awakened around 3am by smoke in my room. Found smoke in Maud's room too, and going to Bristol Room found ceiling in flames. Maud heroically telephoned for fire brigade. I roused Adamson and maids and we all got down. All in nightclothes. No time even to get stockings or socks. Picked up rugs and overcoat and my suit and got across to harness room Sat there 'til dawn, flames lighting up the whole dreadful scene.'

The firefighters suggested the cause had been a blowtorch. The winter of 1947 was so bitter that the pipes inside Nymans had frozen and the family had to resort to blowtorches to defrost the plumbing and warm the house again. It is not known who was using the blowtorch, as it was night-time and many of the family were asleep. It was Leonard Messel who woke to the smell of smoke and alerted his family, who escaped just in time. More than seventy firemen came to battle the blaze but it was too far gone when the fire trucks arrived. The grand house of Nymans burned to the ground.

The next morning a salvage party was organised, combing through the snow and ash for personal treasures and valuables, but little of value remained. Only the garden and a wing of the house survived.

Leonard returned to Nymans on 23 March to assess the damage. His diary entry read: 'I looked at the terrible desolation. It is heart-breaking and shows the folly of human aspirations. One must not love worldly or material things too much.'

Unable to consider rebuilding in the era of post-war shortages, the Messels moved to Holmsted Manor, a few miles away.

Curiously, Maud and Leonard's gardens looked dramatic and almost theatrical with the great ruin of the old house in the middle of them. Maud's climbing roses continued to grow and eventually clothed the ruin and its Gothic arched doorways and stone walls in beautiful blooms. The place became even more romantic in its scarred state.

In due course, Nymans was partly rebuilt, and later became the home of Leonard and Maud's daughter Anne and her second husband, the 6th Earl of Rosse. As Caroline explained, the ruin of Nymans survived, in part, because of the beautiful roses.

'It is an incredible story, really,' she explains. 'The story of how the garden survived the fire in the house, and then the garden, in turn, saved the house from becoming derelict, or razed to the ground, because the family wanted to keep as much of it all intact as possible, is fascinating. It is the ultimate garden folly, I think. The story of how roses saved a ruin.'

In many ways, Nymans was fortunate. Maud's old roses had survived the war, and lived to save the house from being destroyed. Other great houses and gardens, however, faced a dark future. Without any gardeners to look after them, it soon became obvious that many of England's grand gardens were in danger of disappearing, particularly those of national importance. In 1947, the Royal Horticultural Society approached the National Trust with a proposal. Could it add gardens of 'outstanding beauty, design or historic interest' to its portfolio of land and houses of national interest? The National Trust agreed. A garden fund was established to take care of the maintenance of 'works of botanical importance'. In 1948, it took custodianship of the first historic property, Hidcote Manor in Gloucestershire, owned and gardened by Lawrence Johnston.

Soon after, Leonard Messel entered into negotiations with the Trust about Nymans. It, too, passed eventually into the care of the National Trust.

In 1955, Graham Stuart Thomas was appointed gardens advisor to the Trust, a position he held until 1974, overseeing the maintenance of 110 public gardens in England, Wales and Ireland. After he retired, he continued as a consultant to the Trust. However, he was not allowed to advise on Nymans, Bodnant and several other gardens. He was not consulted about Nymans until after 1970.

How do you bloom after a bad year? Or a series of horrific years? How do you find the impetus to keep going, to be positive, to look for the joy in life? So many people wondered this after Covid swept the globe. It felt as though we were all waiting for our lives to bloom again. Waiting for the spring, so we could burst forth joyfully and forget the Covid winters that had left us spent.

When I started rewriting this book, after feeling dissatisfied with it for so long, I found I no longer wanted to write about depressing subjects. We had all had too much negativity in our news and social feeds, and in our lives. I realised I wanted to celebrate everything that was beautiful and joyful and scented and sweet. I wanted to embroider a narrative of stories and create the biographical version of a rose garden, where roses entwined the lines and petals fluttered through the pages.

Others, it seemed, felt the same. People rushed to write books about gardens and nature and wildlife, while others started working in their own gardens, whether grand or small. Nurseries emptied of seedlings, husbands were asked to build raised beds for their newly enthusiastic garden-loving wives, and many roses sold out. The quiet simplicity of digging a hole, planting a young plant, and watching for growth gave many of us something to nurture and look forward to. Just as Vita and others had done during hard times, we put our hands into the soil and looked to the earth for solace. It was strangely restorative.

I began gifting seed packets to friends. It was a small gesture, and I did not mind if those friends tucked the packets away in a drawer for another day. It was simply a way of saying: here, plant these when you're feeling down, it might help. My friends later told me that it did. One of these friends – a neighbour and a keen gardener – came to visit me one day. She told me she had decided to sell her lovely cottage in our street and move away. I was devastated. Why? I asked her. She paused, as if to compose herself, and then she told me that her husband of forty years had come home and told her he was leaving her. And that – only an hour before this terrible conversation – at her annual check-up, her doctor had told her she had early stage dementia. Two emotional bombshells in one morning. My friend did not tell her husband of the dementia diagnosis. She simply nodded at his weak explanation, then cried into her roses when he drove away. A month or so later – it was not long at all – they sold the house and each of them moved into separate accommodation. To this friend's delight – and mine – her new home was in an estate that is known for its gardens. Each of the cottages on this estate has its own garden, and to her joy she was moving into a cottage with one of the largest. Her new garden was in a bad way, she told me, but she also told me she thought she could save it. I had no doubt. But I was still nervous for her. So, one night, I packed a box of seeds for her new project – anemones, peony-shaped poppies, delphiniums, digitalis, agastaches – all in her favourite colour, purple. As I put the last seed packet in the pile, I thought of her circumstances, and I began to cry. I went outside and looked up at the moonlit sky. I wondered if she would still be aware of the flowers and seasons in another year. Another three years? Would she be coherent enough to see the Pompom poppies unfurl? The anemones sway? Would she see that the 'Amazing Grey' poppy really is an amazing grey? Then I remembered: gardening is about hope. These seeds offered not just beauty but the possibility of a future, the possibility of happiness, of a new beginning. My friend needed hope at that moment, even if it was only in the form of a tiny paper packet with the words 'when to sow' marked on the front. I listened to Josh Groban singing that bittersweet Simon & Garfunkel song 'April, Come She Will', and I took the seed packets and I tucked them carefully into a big envelope, with a card that told her how proud I was of her.

We are all going through our quiet battles. Big or small, they weary us. Still, we press on, with hope in our hearts. Like Vita, let us all leave something for others, whether it be roses, words, stories, flowers – or just hope for the future.

In 1945, Constance Spry decided, like many, to start a new life. She was burned out and thought a change of scenery would be beneficial. She also wanted to create a new garden, one where she could focus on the cultivation and preservation of her beloved old roses, which she wanted to bring back into fashion. She found the solution in an idyllic property called Winkfield Place.

Connie had already decided to start a school – not a finishing school but a starter school, a 'beginning school', as she dubbed it – for girls who wanted to learn new skills such as gardening and cooking. Winkfield Place was perfect for this plan. It was a grand Georgian mansion midway between Windsor and Ascot on the outskirts of London. It had everything Connie wanted: room for classes and room to grow flowers, both for her own personal collection and for commercial use in her business. There were seven acres in total, enough for a serious cutting garden, as well as a significant area devoted to old roses. She and her gardeners would plant no fewer than 1,200 rose bushes throughout the property. The estate had been used by the military during the war and it was badly in need of repairs, so Connie negotiated a good price.

Before she left Park Gate House, she and her gardener, Walter Trower, spent several months sorting out how they were going to transport all the old roses to their new home. The cuttings that Walter had taken of many of the old roses, to safeguard their survival, had indeed survived the war but, so too, had the more established modern roses that had been cultivated to supply blooms for Connie's business. Connie had employed a total of seven gardeners during the war years, although six worked part-time and only Walter was full-time while some of the others came from Swanley Horticultural College, with which Connie had a close association. Connie had continued to run Park Gate Farm as a farm and plant nursery through the war years, albeit on a small scale, with most of the flowers going to her business.

In 1945, Graham Stuart Thomas visited Park Gate House one last time before Connie sold it. Together, the two of them walked to the rose garden through the old cherry orchard. Graham was amazed to find that she had amassed one of the best and biggest collections of old roses in the country. He also realised she had many rare specimens of old roses. Clearly, Connie had been collecting as many old roses as Graham and Vita had. And clearly, none of the three rosarians had revealed this to many people. In his *Rose Book*, Graham recorded that Connie was so passionate about her old roses that 'French names flowed from her' until her enthusiasm was contagious. Graham was swept up in her post-war joy. Her interest in and passion for old roses reinforced his view that these plants should be promoted and cherished. For her part, Connie kindly allowed Graham to take cuttings of many of the roses, so he could propagate them, sell them, and write about them for his books.

Eventually, Connie's entire collection of old roses was moved to Winkfield Place, with Graham's help. Once settled in their new home, Connie and Harry (Shav) said goodbye to Park Gate House and their beloved garden. Shav was not happy. He had hoped to retire to Kent. But Connie had the money. She was leading the way. At Winkfield Place, Connie began to devote much of her spare time to the cultivation of old roses. She had been waiting a long time for the right place with the right amount of land, and now that she had found her perfect 'rose farm', there was no stopping her. Like Graham and Vita, her efforts to grow and promote old roses would be instrumental in bringing them back into fashion.

(Side note: in 1947, Connie was asked to create the floral arrangements for Princess Elizabeth's wedding to Philip Mountbatten, Prince of Greece and Denmark. It was an occasion designed to brighten dreary post-war London. Connie arranged urns of English flowers in Westminster Abbey and then used pink and white British-grown carnations to decorate the lunch tables at Buckingham Palace. The princess carried British-grown orchids in a huge, wired bouquet that covered much – but not quite all – of the embroidery on her beautiful dress.)

Sissinghurst's garden had survived the war. The old walls were still intact and so, too, were most of the hedges, thanks to Harold and Vita, who had kept them clipped – an enormous job. Unlike many other gardens, none of Sissinghurst's flower beds had been dug up to grow food – 'there was plenty of room at Sissinghurst for a separate kitchen garden,' explains Troy Scott Smith – and so the perennials and roses would not take much to revive. Harold and Vita had weeded the spring garden too, while Vita had scythed the orchards and pruned the roses. Most importantly of all, the buildings and bricks of the garden walls were still intact. 'The German bombers that flew directly overhead had not succeeded in bombing any part of the garden or buildings,' wrote Helen Champion, Sissinghurst's former assistant head gardener in her wonderful blog about the garden. Photographs taken just after the war show that the orchard was tired but still standing, and the weeds around the South Cottage, where Vita and Harold lived, were rampant but not too high. 'There was plenty to do, but with a proper workforce and knowledgeable gardeners, Sissinghurst could be rescued from its decline,' said Helen.

As Vita later wrote (*House & Garden*, 1950): 'One needs years of patience to make a garden; one needs deeply to love it, in order to endure that patience. One needs optimism and foresight. One has to wait. One has to work hard oneself, sometimes, as I had to work hard, manually, during the war years, cutting all those hedges with shears in my spare time. I hated those hedges, when I looked at my blistered hands; but at the same time I still felt that it had been worthwhile planting them. They were the whole pattern and design and anatomy of the garden; and, as such, were worth any trouble I was willing to take. The rest of the garden just went wild during the war years. We had begun to get it tidy, and then it reverted to the wildness in which we had found it in 1930. We could not cope with it at all. Now it is better.'

In 1946, Sissinghurst's former head gardener Jack Vass returned to work for Vita. She had hired him just before the war and was overjoyed when he returned safely from France. He and the other gardeners began the long process of cutting back the overgrowth that had taken over Sissinghurst. The Herb Garden has suffered most; it had to be completely dug over and replanted. Copper, the chauffeur, helped with garden duties. Everyone pitched in. The moat was cleaned, and the lake dredged. They also began work on the White Garden.

With the return of Jack Vass, her sons and a sense of normality, Vita came back to life. Her spirit and energy returned. Writer Anne Scott-James believed that this period, the post-war years, was probably her peak, both as a plantswoman and as a gardening writer. Horticultural honours were bestowed upon her. In 1946, Vita began writing the celebrated weekly gardening columns for *The Observer*, which continued until 1961 and which were loved by gardeners all over England. She was the Monty Don of her day. People embraced her down-to-earth style, her wit, her humour and her calm, authoritative voice that was instructive without being condescending or dictatorial. Before this, she had contributed occasional articles about living in the country to the *New Statesman* and during the war she had written a series of moving and poignant pieces about Sissinghurst for *Country Life*. But *The Observer* took her voice to a far greater reach of readers. Vita's reputation was soon as great as that of her garden. (Many of Vita's columns are available in books: *In Your Garden, In Your Garden Again* and *More for Your Garden*. There are also articles she wrote for the *Journal* of the RHS and about flowers that caught her fancy.)

One of the subjects Vita was *not* allowed to publish in the original *Observer* columns was a list of nurserymen, seedsman and other growers of plants, possibly because it could have been seen as promoting these businesses. 'Neither *The Observer* nor any other journal could have allowed the "free advertisement" of publishing the names and addresses,' Vita explained. It was a shame, as her contacts were extensive, and quite often included smaller and lesser-known nurseries that would have benefited from the exposure.

One of the nurserymen Vita liked to call on for advice and plants was Graham Stuart Thomas. One day in 1947, Graham drove to Sissinghurst to visit his friend. He later tried to describe her to the American garden writer Anne Raver, who wrote a profile about him for the *New York Times*. He said that Vita was 'very charming, very vague [and] very shy'. It was Vita who had invited Graham to Sissinghurst that day in 1947: she wanted to talk about old roses. She took Graham for a walk down to see the unidentified rose, the ancient Gallica – dramatic, plum-coloured but magenta-edged – that she had found when they first inspected Sissinghurst in 1930, all those years ago. Did Graham know what it was? Graham studied it but was not sure. Having asked Edward Bunyard and now Graham and seeing that both these educated rose growers – her 'Expert' friends as she called them (with a capital 'E') – were stumped by this rose, Vita gleefully named it 'Sissinghurst Castle'. It now rambles over one of the many rose beds in the garden, as well as many other garden beds the world over.

Vita later wrote about this mysterious rose in *House & Garden* magazine in 1950: 'The only thing we found of any interest [during the first inspection of Sissinghurst] was an old Gallica rose, then unknown to cultivation, which is now listed as *gallica* var. Sissinghurst Castle, at 10 shillings a plant by Messrs. Hilling of Chobham [Graham's nursery], to whom I gave some runners. Miss Nancy Lindsay, who is an expert on such matters, says that my old rose is *gallica* 'Tour des Maures', a great rarity ... that is as may be. I do not know whether this shrubby, woody old rose I found ramping here is of any interest at all. I know only that it is fun and interesting to find anything growing on any old site, because you never know what it may turn out to be.'

The mysterious Gallica at Sissinghurst set a newly determined Graham Stuart Thomas on a path to identify roses whose names had become lost or muddled up with other names. He had already been doing this to some extent, but now he was more serious. At the age of thirty-eight, he was a rosarian with a mission.

Graham was still at Hillings nursery. He had worked his way up from foreman to manager, and would remain in this role until 1955. During the war, Hillings had grown potatoes and vegetables to help feed the nation, although Graham later admitted that he and Thomas Hilling had also grown roses. But in 1945 many of the garden beds were again turned over to ornamental plants.

Graham turned his post-war focus to old roses.

Clair Martin, rose curator of Huntington Botanical Gardens in California, later wrote about Graham for the *Los Angeles Times*, in an obituary for the great rosarian. '[Graham Stuart] Thomas set about preserving the heritage of old roses when many of them were on the verge of extinction.' Anne Raver concurred in her obituary for Graham in the *New York Times* in 2003, writing that he began collecting old climbers and shrub roses from private gardens and nurseries during the war. '[After he war] he then propagated them and promoted them in his prose and his pictures.' Graham himself wrote of this time in his life in a piece entitled 'My Favourite Roses' (published later in his life), recalling that he only began collecting old roses after the war. 'It was not until immediately after the Second World War that I too became aware of their beauty,' he wrote.

Anne Raver actually interviewed Graham a few years before he died for a short story in the *New York Times*.' He told her that every time an auction of roses came up for sale, he was there, ready to buy the entire lot. He would then transport them to the extra land near the nursery at Hillings, where they were quietly rehomed.

Charles Quest-Ritson said, however, that this was not *quite* true. It's a good story, and Graham was adept at storytelling, but Charles said Graham did not venture far to find his old roses. 'He liked people to think that he amassed a collection of old roses by visiting grand old ladies in their great estates and winkling out their ancient cultivars, but it is not true. Most of his roses came from collections that Hilling bought.'

While this is no doubt true, Graham still set out on rose-hunting adventures across England. Vita also began travelling around England, ostensibly to visit her friends, but also to see their gardens and perhaps take cuttings, if they would allow it.

It was not easy to travel around England during this time. Fuel, building supplies and many other things were still rationed. (Britain introduced petrol rationing just three weeks after war with Germany was officially declared in September 1939, and the rationing continued until 1950.) Some aristocrats and landowners of large estates and agricultural concerns were given more petrol than others, because they had tractors and machinery to run. James Lees-Milne once wrote of how the Duke of Wellington met him at the station, on 15 April 1944, when he caught the 1.15 to Reading. 'Gerry Wellington met me at the station in his small car, for he gets twenty gallons a month for being a duke.' It is likely that Vita received additional fuel for the farm vehicles at Sissinghurst, while Graham received addition petrol allowances for his nursery work. I asked Charles Quest-Ritson about this, and he agreed. 'People working with the government during the Second World War were given more petrol allowances. They were known as 'Reserved Occupations'. Nurserymen were in this category. That's how people such as Graham – and indeed Vita – were able to drive around the countryside, while others were bound to what their petrol rations allowed.'

Vita loved these botanical road trips. She replaced her wartime Buick with a lovely new Austin (which would, in time, be replaced by a Jaguar – although her grandson Adam says there was also a series of Rolls-Royces that sat in the garage), and this gave her an excuse to go motoring through the English countryside, visiting gardens and gardening friends. She loved driving into the green hills of Gloucestershire, Herefordshire, Wiltshire and Devon.

On one of these trips, in June 1949, she stopped by Hidcote Manor Garden, where Nancy Lindsay, the daughter of the renowned garden designer Norah Lindsay, showed her around Lawrence Johnston's famous garden. Johnston had gone to live in France after the war, where he had a garden, and had intended to leave Hidcote to his friend Norah Lindsay. But Norah had died in 1948, so Johnston had left the garden to the National Trust, run by a management committee, of which Norah's daughter Nancy was a member. Nancy, having grown up at her mother's extraordinary estate, Sutton Courtenay (which had been sold by this time), was as avid a gardener as her mother and Vita. She offered Vita anything she desired from the rose collection at Hidcote. According to Jane Brown in her garden biography *Vita's Other World*, Vita was offered (and gratefully took) the rare mauve 'Tour de Malakoff', the precious maroon 'Nuits de Young', and the double golden briar from Persia, *Rosa haemispherica*. In this way, says Jane Brown, Vita gathered her precious horticultural treasures, driving around England in her beloved Austin car.

Vita's visit to Hidcote was the beginning of a new friendship with Nancy Lindsay that was primarily built on roses. From then on, Nancy wrote Vita long rambling letters about roses. And Vita, always the diligent letter writer, replied in kind. It became an epistolary friendship, built on vivid descriptions of heritage roses.

Back at Hillings, Graham was busy with his new collections of old roses. By 1948, he had assembled what was arguably one of the greatest collections of old roses in England.

Graham's efforts in saving old roses made Connie realise she needed a succession plan for her own old roses. She asked him if, when the time came, he would take some of her collection. He said yes. He told her that he would also help propagate them before that time came. (Eventually he would take on Connie's entire rose collection.)

According to Charles Quest-Ritson, Graham had acquired and trialled some 1,600 different roses by this time. However, he decided that only about 250 were worth saving. Many of the rest, claimed Charles, in an interview for this biography, are now extinct. This is because Graham was not a conservationist. Not yet. He was just a nurseryman and a businessman, trying to select the best varieties to sell. Once he had determined which of the old roses would do their best, Graham listed them and then launched his 'Old Garden Roses' catalogue. This catalogue was a fantastic sourcebook of glorious old Gallicas, Damasks, Moss roses and other varieties – and Graham promoted them as being an 'upmarket' line. As such, buyers had to pay a premium. At the time, the new Hybrid Tea roses cost twelve shillings and sixpence each (or 12/6). For his old roses, though, Graham charged fifteen shillings. As Charles said: Graham was an astute businessman as much as a rosarian.

However, gardeners looking for plants to grow were worried about the fact that old roses flowered only once. What was the point, said some, when Hybrid Teas were repeat flowering? Graham pointed to the old roses' ravishing forms, their extraordinary beauty – so much like the roses of old paintings – and their names: the Duchesse de Montebello and Empress Josephine. (The latter rose has a working name – it has still not definitely been identified. Graham called it 'Empress Josephine' because was a good selling name.) The middle classes were soon hooked.

There was an issue, though – one that Charles and Brigid Quest-Ritson identified and discussed with me in an interview for this biography. 'Hillings nursery had bought more than a thousand old roses from various places, including auctions. The nursery had also acquired 1,200 roses from Beckwith and they had also bought roses from Daisy Hill nursery. I think they had collected around 1,600 of these rare old roses in total, by this time,' said Charles. 'Thomas Hilling and Graham planned to propagate and sell these old roses to the opinion-makers, the style-setters, the fashionable people, whose influence would filter down and thus increase the demand for his roses.' The business plan to make old roses fashionable again was a joint effort between the two men, said Charles. 'In 1945 or 1946, Hillings released their first list or catalogue of old roses. But the interesting thing is, the catalogue only had 300 or so old roses for sale.'

Which prompts the question: what happened to the rest of the 1,600 roses? What happened to the 1,300 old roses that were left? Were they simply discarded?

Charles paused as he told this story, to let the truth sink in. 'That is the shocking fact,' he said, matter-of-factly.

Like Charles, I was mystified by this. How did Graham choose which roses to propagate and sell in the nursery's catalogues? Which ones did he leave off the list? Which ones were relegated to the 'Do Not Propagate' pile? I asked Charles and Brigid Quest-Ritson this, and Brigid intervened. 'It is difficult to know how Graham chose them. One doesn't know what the discrepancies were.'

It seems – and this is the incredible thing – that these 1,300 or so old roses were discontinued. Discarded and now likely out of stock, given that most roses fade from the lists of nurseries within – say – fifteen years of their introduction, as the rose trade is posited on novelty.

Discriminating editing aside, Graham Stuart Thomas soon found success with his catalogues of old roses. He also began to influence other notable rose growers, including Peter Beales, who worked with him for a short time at Hillings. (Peter Beales's nursery today is still one of the best sources of old roses in Great Britain.)

The popularity of old roses was soon rising again.

15

Rose-coloured Glasses

'[One] must discard the idea that roses must be limited to certain accepted and accustomed colours, and to welcome the less familiar purples and lilacs, and the striped, flaked, mottled variations which recall the old Dutch flower-paintings; to approach them, in fact, with open and unprejudiced eyes, and also with a nose that esteems the true scent of a rose warmed by the sun.'

Vita Sackville-West

The 1950s were a challenging time for old roses. Modern new roses such as Floribundas and Hybrid Teas were being introduced by breeders all the time. According to Jennifer Potter, who wrote the wonderful, well-researched book *The Rose,* many old roses, especially the old shrub roses, had virtually disappeared from most nurserymen's lists by the 1950s, though a small number of nurseries, including Hillings, Constance Spry and Hilda Murrell's nursery, still sold old roses.

Seeing this trend, Vita, Graham and people such as nurserywoman Hilda Murrell stepped up their efforts to promote old roses. Vita knew that if she wrote about a particular rose, interest in that rose would increase. As Anne Scott-James noted: 'Once she had begun to write about gardening, Vita's influence became profound.' For example, on 28 May 1950, Vita wrote: 'The roses are coming out and I hope everybody will take the opportunity of seeing as many of the *old* roses as possible.' Vita had deliberately italicised the word 'old' for emphasis.

In turn, nurserymen and women knew that a reference to a particular plant in a Vita Sackville-West article or broadcast would create an instant demand. In fact, Hilda Murrell's nursery received so many visitors from Vita's recommendations that in 1952 Hilda decided to visit her at Sissinghurst, ostensibly to thank Vita for sending so many customers her way but also to see the Sissinghurst rose garden that had become so famous. The two women immediately became friends, just as Vita and Connie had done, and not just because they liked the exact same roses. (Hilda also helped Vita with her plant choices for the White Garden.) Later, when Vita's friend Alvilde Lees-Milne began creating her garden at Roquebrune in the South of France in 1954, Vita sent her one of Hilda's catalogues, with recommendations noted alongside various roses.

Two of Vita's rose catalogues from Hilda Murrell's nursery still exist today, marked with crosses for the roses Vita wanted to buy. Three crosses meant a 'yes'. The three-cross roses include 'Félicité et Perpétue', 'Climbing Étoile de Hollande', 'Lawrence Johnston', 'Blanc Double de Coubert' and 'Charles Mallerin'. Other roses that had marks (but not quite the 'multiple cross' tick of approval) were 'Fantin-Latour', 'Comtesse du Caÿla', 'Masquerade', 'Paul's Lemon Pillar', 'Tour de Malakoff', 'Cardinal de Richelieu', 'Charles de Mills', 'Maître École', 'Rose à Parfum de l'Haÿ', 'The Garland', 'Complicata' and 'Souvenir du Docteur Jamain'.

The last rose is interesting because Vita claimed to have discovered it, saved it from becoming endangered, and helped to reintroduce it to nursery lists such as those published by Hillings and Murrells. As Vita later wrote: 'I am rather proud of having rescued it from extinction.' She then elaborated on the story of its discovery in an article in *House & Garden* in 1950. 'It was a very deep red, fading to purple, and with the strongest rose scent that ever a rose had. They [the nursery in Penshurst where she found it] were rather contemptuous of it; did not even know its name; hadn't even bothered to propagate it. They said I could have the old plant if I liked to risk moving it. I risked it; it bore the move, and has turned out to be 'Souvenir du Docteur Jamain', a climbing Hybrid Perpetual almost lost to cultivation. It strikes easily from cuttings, and now has a lot of children, both in my own garden and Messrs. Hilling's – at a price.'

Another time she wrote of this rose: 'I found him growing against the office wall of an old nursery. No one knew what he was, no one seemed to care; no one knew his name; no one had troubled to propagate him. "Could I dig him up," I asked? "Well, if you like to risk it," they said, shrugging their shoulders. "It is a very old plant, with a woody stiff root." I risked it. 'Docteur Jamain' survived his removal, and now has a flourishing progeny in my garden, and also on the market of a certain rosarian to whom I gave it.' (She is clearly referring to Graham Stuart Thomas.)

Vita's friendships with these knowledgeable old-rose lovers, and her botanical road trips to find rare and old roses in the gardens and estates of friends all over England, certainly helped her search for roses. Harold was working at Windsor Castle on his biography of George V, so Vita had ample time on her hands to embark on her horticultural travels.

On 14 June 1951, Vita took Harold to see Connie's garden at Winkfield Place. They all had lunch, then walked around the rose garden and the field of flowers for cutting. Connie gave Vita cuttings of her old roses. Vita took these precious roses from her friend and returned to Sissinghurst to find room for them in her own Rose Garden, which by summer of 1951 was reaching perfection. The garden, argues Jane Brown in *Vita's Other World*, was Vita's 'spiritual home', a room as expressive of her personality as her writing room. 'Her collection was at its peak during the fifties. And she [Vita] must take much credit for showing off the roses that first her old friend Edward Bunyard and later Graham Stuart Thomas wrote about. From where we stand now, the success of old roses owes a lot to her.'

Vita's roses and the garden at Sissinghurst became so famous in the 1950s that its reputation extended all the way to Buckingham Palace. The Queen Mother's private secretary wrote and asked if Her Majesty could visit. Of course, said Vita, and invited her for lunch. On Wednesday, 4 June 1952, a beautiful summer's day when the roses had just started their first flush, the Queen Mother arrived. Together, she and Vita wandered slowly around the garden – Vita had dressed in a skirt especially for the occasion (the Queen was in silk) – and talked about gardening. The Queen Mother was herself a keen gardener, as the King had been. King George VI had died on 6 February that year, and the Queen, newly widowed, was probably grateful to be out and about, visiting gardens.

Vita was constantly surprised by all the attention that she and Sissinghurst received, not just in Britain but in America and Australia and other parts of the gardening world. She always thought she would be a celebrated poet and writer. She probably never imagined that it would be her garden that brought her international recognition. She accepted it all the same. 'Fame', as Jane Brown, put it, 'had settled lightly and serenely on Vita's world.'

Vita continued to order more old roses, even as the Rose Garden and other borders and beds and walls filled up with them. Parcels constantly arrived from Graham at Hillings, Nancy Lindsay at Hidcote Manor, Hilda Murrell at Shrewsbury, and other nurseries.

In 1954, the garden was glorious. Thousands of people passed through it. On New Year's Eve in 1954, Harold and Vita hosted a party – a rare occasion at Sissinghurst – and it, too, felt celebratory. The couple were beset by health issues – Harold had suffered two mild strokes and given up gardening – although he continued to weed the Nuttery, one of his favourite parts of the garden, into the 1960s. And Vita's arthritis became worse until she, too, could not write, and found it hard to hold a gardening tool. The two became close during this period. It was as though they knew their years and seasons, their springs and summers together were limited.

Graham Thomas, meanwhile, was also madly propagating as many old roses as fast as he could source them. In 1955, he decided to leave Hillings nursery, where he had begun as foreman and finished as manager, and had contributed so much to horticulture. He moved to Sunningdale Nurseries in Windlesham, Surrey, where he was employed as the manager. (When he finally retired in 1973, he would be an associate director.) Sunningdale was known as one of most highly regarded nurseries in the country. This was partly because of its magnificent collection of old roses, but mostly because of its beautiful rhododendrons. Graham was focused on the roses.

According to Brent Elliott in his RHS book *The Rose*, Graham was constantly 'seeking out surviving specimens of old roses, to be redistributed through his Sunningdale Nursery. His search increasingly began to attract public interest. After the example of Vita Sackville-West at Sissinghurst, the idea of a garden that did not merely include, but was devoted solely to, old roses began to spread.'

In 1955, Graham decided to write a book about old roses called *The Old Shrub Roses*. The publisher was J. M Dent & Sons Ltd. *Old Shrub Roses* was not Graham's first rose-writing project. He had previously written a booklet called *The Manual of Shrub Roses*, describing all the varieties, with advice on cultivation. In the foreword he described the booklet's aim: 'To bring forth these lovely things from retirement.' But *Old Shrub Roses* was his first commercial success.

Vita Sackville West wrote the foreword to *The Old Shrub Roses*, and – true to Vita form, it was memorably poetic. *Old Shrub Roses* was the first of many successful books for Graham, who went on to write *Shrub Roses of Today* (1962), which focused on modern varieties that looked like old roses, to try and win cynics over to non-standard roses, and *Climbing Roses Old and New* (1965), which was enhanced by the author's glorious drawings and paintings. There were other books, too, but it was thanks to these encyclopaedic works that Graham's influence soon extended to Europe and beyond, to the United States. They provided much-needed information about the history and extent of old roses at a time when these varieties were being overshadowed by their repeat-flowering and showier cousins, the Hybrid Teas and Floribundas. As a result of Graham's books, gardeners all over the world began to fall back in love with old roses.

The late, great British rose breeder David Austin acknowledged Graham's contribution to old roses in his own book *The Heritage of the Rose* (1988). 'Graham Stuart Thomas did more than just preserve these roses,' wrote David Austin. 'He changed the way we looked at them.' 'The forms and colours of old garden roses are generally more pleasing. The perfumes of old roses are richer, too', he said. David Austin and Graham travelled to Paris together in June 1953 to visit the rose gardens. It seems to be the only occasion in which Graham went to the European mainland.

The 1950s were productive years for these workaholic rosarians but they were also exhausting. Connie worked as hard as she had always done, tending to her flower shop in London, lecturing around the country, growing her old roses at Winkfield Place, teaching her students how to cook and garden, and being actively involved with the Chelsea Flower Show.

Then, in 1953 came her greatest commission. Connie was asked to supply and arrange the flowers for the coronation of Queen Elizabeth II. It was a huge undertaking, involving choosing flowers for Westminster Abbey, as well as the flowers for the entire processional route and for Buckingham Palace. It was perhaps the highlight of her career. The highlight of her life.

Connie worked right up until the day she died. On 3 January 1960, she slipped on the stairs at Winkfield Place while arranging flowers. She died an hour later.

The following year, in tribute to Connie, both Graham Stuart Thomas and David Austin named the first of Austin's home-bred roses 'Constance Spry'. It is considered the foundation of David Austin's

'English Rose' series. 'Constance Spry' was bred from a cross between a Gallica and a Floribunda, and was (and still is) a beautiful semi-climber with glorious pink petals and a strong, sweet myrrh fragrance.

Two months after Connie's death, on 8 March 1960, Maud Messel also passed away. She was 84. It was early spring, just as the yellow daffodils were breaking through Nymans' green lawns. Leonard, her husband, had died in 1953. He never returned to live at Nymans after the fire. He bequeathed the gardens to the National Trust. Maud's rose garden continued to flourish. It is still just as splendid today.

The Times published an obituary the day after Maud's death. It included the following paragraph: 'In her later years, Mrs Messel was more than the legendary great lady of an archaic past. Certainly, her exquisite manner and presence belonged to a different age from ours. Her iridescent, almost gossamer-like beauty was that of the tenderly nurtured exotic than the wild hedgerow flower. Her gentle voice, however, spoke from the depths of unfeigned compassion and understanding. And beneath her apparent fragility lay a strength of character, an invincibility of courage, and an insatiable fund of interest in all those around her.'

Two months after Maud's death, her grandson Antony Armstrong-Jones married the Queen's sister, Princess Margaret, in a lavish ceremony. Maud would have adored it.

16

Passing the Secateurs

'I like being outside by myself. And I like digging.'

Sibylle Kreutzberger, former head gardener (with
Pamela Schwerdt) at Sissinghurst Castle Garden

In 1959, Vita became ill. She began suffering pain. It was the un-diagnosed beginnings of cancer.

She often stayed in bed for days – which was uncharacteristic of her, especially during the balmy afternoons of summer when her roses were blooming. Harold and her friends took turns leaving roses and flowers at her bedroom door. They could not bear to disturb her on these days. When she recovered enough to go back out into the garden, although not to work in it, Vita decided to appoint a new head gardener to help. In the end she appointed two.

Pamela Schwerdt (who was born in 1931, the year after Vita found Sissinghurst) and Sibylle Kreutzberger had met at the Waterperry School of Horticulture for Ladies, where they quickly established a friendship and lived together for the rest of their lives. Sibylle and Pam wanted to establish their own nursery but, with no money or land, their first issue was to find somewhere affordable to cultivate the plants. They placed an advertisement in *The Times'* personal column, asking if anyone might be willing to lease two acres. At the same time Pam wrote to Vita Sackville-West, who was at that time *The Observer's* gardening correspondent. Vita replied, suggesting that she try Wye College, in Kent, but then added a postscript: She needed a head gardener for Sissinghurst – would she be interested? Pam replied: 'Yes, but we are two.'

To begin with, Pam and Sibylle were not sure about Vita, or the jobs they were being asked to do. They later joked that they did not know who was interviewing whom, but they decided to take the position and moved into a cottage opposite the oasthouses.

Sibylle became the propagator, and Pam took on the duties of a conventional head gardener. After gardening was done for the day, they would go back to the cottage, have their evening meal, and then do paperwork. There were four under-gardeners to assist them – all men – and the two new head gardeners knew they had achieved a rare thing:

two female gardeners in a top job in horticulture. Sibylle acknowledged their luck as late as 2006, when she looked back on those first years in the job. 'When we first went to Sissinghurst, people used to point at us as though we were baboons at the zoo.'

Their jobs included displaying plants for sale outside the gate. For this they used a yellow cart painted with pictures of Sissinghurst. Boxes, painted yellow to match the cart, were used as staging for the plants.

Vita rarely interrupted their work. And they rarely interrupted hers. Vita's health was still not good, although she was able to walk around the garden. She preferred to be alone in her tower room, writing. Thursdays was '*Observer* day', when she would shut herself away to write her gardening column for the newspaper.

Among the visitors who came to Sissinghurst in 1961 were Princess Margaret, Cecil Beaton, Cyril Connolly and Elizabeth Bowen. Vita, whose strength came and went, also gave a lecture on roses to the RHS at Vincent Square.

Vita's final article on gardening was written in December 1961. It was on roses and pruning and entitled 'My Roses Thrive on a Touch of Neglect.' In it, she gently suggested that roses should not be pruned heavily but left to grow in romantic abandon.

That was Vita – living on the edge of conformity, both in life and in horticulture, right until the very end.

17

Nearing the End of
the Garden Path

'For the last forty years of my life, I have broken my
back, my fingernails, and sometimes my heart in the
practical pursuit of my favourite occupation.'

Vita Sackville-West, *The Observer*, 1953

V ita was intensely aware of the seasons, as most gardeners are. She followed the weather patterns, the movements of the moon, the subtle nuances of each month and season. On the last day of 1961, she wrote: 'Horribly cold. Starts to snow. By evening it is inches deep. I go back to the tower.' There in the tower, listening to the news, she heard that more snow and frost were forecast. 'We have champagne for dinner, and I hope that 1962 will be nicer than 1961.' Unfortunately, 1962 would not be a better year. Not for Vita. She was dying. She did not say anything to anyone. For once she did not have the words. She may not have realised the extent of the seriousness of her abdominal cancer, but she knew was very ill. She certainly did not make a fuss.

As Vita's health deteriorated in early 1962, she must have felt not only fear for herself but also fear for her garden, deep in her gardener's heart. She would have known Harold was also ageing, and while she trusted her team to continue with Sissinghurst's responsibilities, she must have felt – like all gardeners – a little anxious about relinquishing control. As she continued to carry out literary appointments during those first months of 1962, she probably knew it would be the last March she might ever see. The last April. The last May.

What did Vita think, as she contemplated the path ahead of her? Did she wander her garden in the lilac hours of twilight, thinking of Heaven and Earth? Did she remember when she first saw Sissinghurst, on that rainy April day in 1930? Did she contemplate how far she had come? Often, it is only when gardeners look back at photos of the first year they arrived at a place that they appreciate the improvement they have made on the landscape. One of the most poignant things Vita wrote in 1961 was a letter to Harold, which she penned in November. She said, in a now-famous quote: 'We have done our best, and made a garden where none was.'

In January 1962, Vita began suffering from internal haemorrhages, which she managed to conceal. Knowing it could be their last trip, she agreed to go on a cruise with Harold, to the Caribbean. Vita spent most of the trip in her cabin, reading. She was afraid to go out in public, to sit on seats or indeed on her clothes in case she had another bleed. When the couple finally arrived home in England and took the Pullman train from Southampton to London, she was mortified to see there was a stain where she had been sitting. She had made it all the way around the Caribbean without leaving evidence of her illness. Did Harold notice the mark on the seat? If he did, he certainly did not say anything. A diplomat to the end.

The couple finally arrived home at Sissinghurst, and for Vita it was a poignant homecoming. She knew she would never go travelling again. Vita, as eloquent as ever, wrote: 'The orchard is misty-mauve with Tomasinianus; parrotia flowering as never before.' She also added: 'I feel really ill.' It is an honest postscript that shows she is aware of how terribly sick she really is.

Vita was soon admitted to hospital in London, where she underwent a hysterectomy. During her operation, the surgeons confirmed she had advanced abdominal cancer. After the surgery, a surgeon found Harold, sat him down, and told him there was little they could do. Harold was inconsolable. He always thought he would die first.

Vita and Harold stayed by each other's side after the surgeon delivered the news, just as they had always done. Vita told Harold she wanted to leave the hospital. She wanted to go home. To her beloved garden.

On 25 May, Harold told his London secretary to put all his meetings on hold and went home to Sissinghurst to be with his wife.

On Saturday, 2 June 1962 – the start of the rose season – Vita lay in bed in the Priest's House. She had moved from the South Cottage into an upstairs room in the Priest's House to make life easier for everyone, especially her carers. Vita was weak. She knew her time was near. She turned to her devoted dog Glen, a golden retriever, who had nosed his way in, and whispered quietly to him. Then she closed her eyes.

Outside, on the pink brick walls, Vita's roses were just coming into bloom. Harold picked some of her favourite roses and laid them on her bed. One of Vita's carers and friends, Ursula, had already opened the window. With the windows open wide, Vita's spirit was once more with her garden. She was seventy years of age. Her garden at Sissinghurst was almost half as old – 32 years. Garden and gardener had matured together.

In the following weeks, the 'Madame Alfred Carrière' rose that Vita had planted when she and Harold bought Sissinghurst suddenly unfurled into flower. The rest of the roses followed. It was as if they were celebrating her life in bloom. Like a botanical orchestra playing a great, glorious, garlanded tribute to their conductor.

At Vita's funeral, parts of her poem *The Land* were read. Many years later, in 1993, English Heritage put up a blue plaque on the front of Vita and Harold's former home at 182 Ebury Street, Belgravia, London, where she had written *The Land*. English Heritage acknowledged the contribution the duo had made to gardening in the wording of the plaque. The plaque simply said their names and below them: 'Writers and Gardeners lived here.' Vita once recalled that she had 'been very happy there' at Ebury Street. It was, she said, 'the only period in my life when I achieved anything like popularity'. How pleased Vita would be to know her garden is now one of the most famous gardens in the world.

That winter, the winter of 1962-3, Britain endured one of the longest and coldest spells of weather that the country had ever seen. Snow started to fall in Kent on Boxing Day and it did not stop for the next ten weeks. The 'Big Freeze of 1963' broke temperature records. It is still considered the worst winter in modern British history. Sissinghurst suffered many plant losses. It was a good thing Vita did not live to see it. She would have been worried for her roses.

In 1967 Harold and Vita's son Nigel Nicolson, struggling with an inheritance tax bill that had been due since his mother's death, gave Sissinghurst to the National Trust with a proviso: he and his family could go on living there rent-free. Thanks to the National Trust, with which Vita had been involved, many of Britain's greatest houses and gardens, such as Sissinghurst, are looked after forever and open to the public for all to enjoy.

Pamela and Sybille were kept on as head gardeners. By the time they retired in 1990 they had assembled a talented team of gardeners who ensured that Sissinghurst's reputation would carry on into the twenty-first century.

Vita's garden would continue to be loved for decades. Head gardener Troy Scott Smith, in an interview for this biography, feels that Sissinghurst's garden is one of the world's greatest works of art. Vita's grandson, the writer Adam Nicolson, agrees. In an article for the *New York Times Style Magazine* in October 2013, he also called it 'one of the greatest English works of art of the 20th century'. And now, thanks to Vita, Harold, the family and also the National Trust, it will be preserved for future generations.

Vita Sackville-West always wanted to be a poetess, a *poĕtria*, a poet laureate. She wrote superb poetry, but it was never her true strength. It was never her métier. Instead, she became one of the world's great gardeners, and a defender of old roses. She also became, without intending to, something of a celebrity. Towards the end of her life, she accepted her unexpected fame. In fact, she was often quietly pleased whenever an organisation or someone with authority recognised her talents. When she heard that the garden at Herstmonceux in Sussex had been planted according to the suggestions given in her broadcast talks, she was deeply touched. 'I felt I had not lived in vain,' she later noted. How moving it is to realise that this woman – a woman who seemingly had everything: a marvellous garden, a loving husband, devoted friends and lovers, servants, a successful career, even a Rolls-Royce and a writing tower – would still be brought to silence by the fact that her garden philosophies and ideas had quietly influenced others.

Isabel Bannerman wrote a story about romantic gardens for the *Telegraph* newspaper in February 2020. It could have referred to Sissinghurst. 'I don't think a romantic garden can be "designed",' wrote Isabel. 'What makes you breathless or blood-rushed in a garden is the humanity that went into it; the passion; the tender care; the reason and the belief that it could work. Real and romantic gardens are not an act of conspicuous consumption, they are about triumph in the face of adversity, about wit and love. Romantic love is about wanting to make a patch with someone, the desire to look after each other and nurture flowers and fruit, and maybe babies, together and generously. The best gardens are about giving and loving.'

That describes Sissinghurst to a T.

It is a garden of romance. A garden of grace. A garden of love.

18

Mottisfont – a Grand Garden of Old Roses

'We are now at the garden door...'

Graham Stuart Thomas, *An English Rose Garden*

U nlike Sissinghurst, the fate of Graham Stuart Thomas's roses
was uncertain.

In 1955, Graham had decided to leave T. Hilling and
Co. after two decades at the helm of the successful nursery, and moved
to Sunningdale Nurseries in Windlesham, Surrey. He was appointed
manager before becoming associate director. He finally retired from
Sunningdale and from nursery work in the summer of 1972. He was 63
years old but he still felt young. And he liked to be outside, among plants
and gardens. What could he do?

There was another issue to contend with. Sunningdale, under his
management, had amassed more than two hundred old and rare roses.
Where would they go? Where can a person plant hundreds of roses?
According to Charles and Brigid Quest-Ritson, Graham arranged for
a representative collection to go to the Royal National Rose Society
garden near St Albans, to see if that would be an option.

It was around this time that Maud Russell entered the picture.
Maud lived in the magnificent Mottisfont Abbey, a former Augustinian
priory in Hampshire. (Mottisfont means 'the moot' or 'meeting place by
the fountain', and probably stems from its origins in mediaeval times.)
Perhaps aware of her mortality, Maud had contacted the National Trust
to see if they could take it on and preserve it. Negotiations continued
until 1957, when the grounds and gardens, together with the estate,
were transferred to the Trust. Maud Russell continued to live there for
another fifteen years.

Mottisfont's walled garden was not being fully used at the time.
It's an enormous space, so this is understandable. It was – and is – a
wonderful place to wander; enclosed on all sides by high brick walls,
and sheltered from the elements. In short, the perfect place to grow
roses. 'Few better sites could be found for a garden of old roses,' Graham
wrote in his 1991 book, *An English Rose Garden*. Graham also wrote

about the idea for a rose garden in 1972. 'Mrs Russell intimated her desire to relinquish the tenancy of these two gardens [at Mottisfont]. It was just after I had given up managership of Sunningdale Nurseries, Surrey, where I had collected all the roses I could find of the ancestral specials. The National Trust decided at the same time to make a collection of these period pieces, the result being that Mottisfont was chosen to be their home. The scheme in general appealed to the members of the Winchester Centre of the Trust, who subscribed enough money to purchase all of the roses.'

Graham was the Gardens Advisor for the National Trust at this time, and it has long been accepted that he was the one who suggested Mottisfont's walled garden be devoted to roses. But Charles Quest-Ritson says it's not as straightforward as that. (And it never is, with such a complicated handover.) However, Graham did have a large role to play in the planting scheme of the garden. After decades of living amongst the petals and scent of old roses, he was an expert in them.

According to Charles Quest-Ritson, the Trust bought all the roses from Mottisfont from various nurseries, including Sunningdale. However, the gardeners had a challenging start to the project. The soil in the old garden was stony and hard and hungry for nutrients. There was also no access through the narrow arches for machinery, so all the compost and manure had to be brought in by barrowload, much of which was done by Mottisfont's head gardener David Stone, to whom Graham Stuart Thomas dedicated *An English Rose Garden*.

In 1997, the garden writer Anne Raver travelled to Mottisfont to meet Graham and walk around the garden to see the old roses with him. She was there to write a story for the *New York Times*. It was June, so the old roses should have been at their peak flowering but this particular June was one of the wettest on record, according to the British Meteorological Office, and consequently, the plants were looking bedraggled. Graham was devastated, by both the bad timing and the state of the roses. 'The roses are all brown!' he said mournfully at the time. Nevertheless, Graham, who was 88 years of age, led Anne briskly to the 'Gallica Officinalis' rose, the famous apothecaries' rose, whose crimson petals hold their fragrance when dried, or made into a jam. He then showed her 'Madame Hardy', a ravishing Damask rose. He explained that the 'Tuscany' rose was not purple in colour but 'murrey', which meant mulberry. And he led her to *Rosa gallica* – 'the great-grandparent of all roses', he said. By the end of the wet tour, Anne was enthralled. And so were the readers of the *New York Times*. When the story, entitled 'So the Roses May Bloom Forever', was published on 17 July 1997, Graham Stuart Thomas – and old roses – found thousands of new fans.

By the 1970s, Graham was the recipient of many prestigious awards. He had been given the Royal Horticultural Society's Veitch Memorial Medal and the Victoria Medal of Honour, and would later receive the Garden Writers' Guild Lifetime Achievement Award, among many other accolades. However, he declared that of all the things he had achieved in his life, he was most proud of his collection of old roses at Mottisfont Abbey. He called this garden a masterpiece. 'I like to think that the rose's pomp will be displayed far into the future at Mottisfont,' he wrote in his notes. He hoped it would also be the place 'where my work of some 30 years collecting ... will not be set at naught'.

In one corner of Mottisfont lies a wooden seat and shelter, where Graham would sit and hold court on hot days in June until only a few years before his death in 2003. Visitors would bring him roses to identify and ask him questions on cultivation. 'His precise, rather schoolmasterly voice dispensed advice and encouragement with all the charm and authority that were the hallmarks of his professional career,' said Charles Quest-Ritson. It is still an idyllic place to sit, shaded from the sun, with the late flowering 'Sander's White Rambler' bowered around you.

Graham Stuart Thomas spent his final years in a small house, called Briar Cottage, where the number of awards for his horticultural work almost crowded out everything else in the living room. The most notable of them was the Order of the British Empire, which was presented to him in 1975 for his work for the National Trust. His front and back gardens at Briar Cottage displayed about 1,500 varieties of plants, including twenty different roses, as well as assorted climbers that covered the fences and the walls of the house. He had become so well known in the rose world that he received eight or ten inquiries a day, from as far as California and Australia. He promptly wrote thank-you letters to each person – in longhand.

Graham died of pneumonia on 17 April 2003, aged 94 (although some sources state he died on 3 April, which was his birthday). He closed his eyes just as the spring bulbs were in full flower. After he died, newspapers in London and New York published lengthy obituaries, many describing him as the 'English botanist best known for his work with garden roses'. The *Los Angeles Times* wrote: 'Graham Stuart Thomas, a horticulturalist, author, and botanical artist … was considered by many garden experts as one of the most influential gardeners of the 20th century.' Most of the writers mentioned his books – which numbered nineteen by the time he died. But mostly they talked about the roses. As *The Guardian* newspaper wrote in May 2003: 'He is owed a huge debt by gardeners for preserving the horticultural heritage of the nation.'

Graham Stuart Thomas achieved a great many things in his long life. He helped to restore the gardens and grounds of more than one hundred historic houses when he served as advisor to the National Trust. But he is perhaps best remembered for his work with old garden roses. As Clair Martin, rose curator at the Huntington Botanical Gardens in San Marino put it in the *Los Angeles Times*: '[Graham Stuart] Thomas set about preserving the heritage of old roses when many of them were on the verge of extinction.' And as *The Guardian* continued in its obituary: '[Graham's] thinking paved the way for several plant conservation movements.' He was 'one of the world's outstanding gardeners and, as a historian and practitioner, he is owed a huge debt by gardeners for preserving the horticultural heritage of the nation, and changing our attitude to using plants.'

19

Finding Vita's Lost Roses

'The most noteworthy thing about gardeners is that they are always optimistic, always enterprising, and never satisfied. They always look forward to doing something better than they have ever done before.'

Vita Sackville-West

The late, great gardener Geoff Hamilton once said that 'seedsmen reckon that their stock in trade is not seeds at all … it is optimism.' This may explain why, during those dark years of war, Vita, Graham, Connie and indeed many others in Great Britain clung to their spades, their seed packets, their humble terracotta pots and their hope. These gardeners found solace in creating small spaces of beauty, of fertility, of flowers they could pick and bring inside, to help them forget there was a war on. And although many roses were dug up to make way for vegetables – a necessary move during wartime so that families had food on their tables – people still found space for them. Roses – and many other flowers – were squished beside potatoes, beans, broccoli, even cabbages. As Vita wrote: 'The gardening papers have all been urging us not to neglect our flowers in favour of our vegetables. Their contention is that man cannot live by potatoes and onions alone, but that his spiritually aesthetic need is as great as his physical.' It was a similar philosophy to that of American environmentalist John Muir, whose is often quoted by gardeners (especially the younger generation who share such things on social media): 'Everybody needs beauty as well as bread, places to play and pray in, where nature may heal and cheer, and give strength to body and soul alike'.

Years after Vita's death, Anne Scott-James wrote that Vita's writing had changed 'the face of English gardening [more] than any other writing since Robinson's *The Flower Garden*'. Anne was right. Vita may not have achieved the fame she so longed for as a poet and a novelist but she created something just as extraordinary for the world to enjoy. She created a garden of grandeur and grace.

More than sixty years after Vita's death (2022 was the sixtieth anniversary of her passing), and 130 years after her birth, Sissinghurst is still one of the leading gardens in the world. But there's a curious and fascinating postscript to this story. In 2013, Sissinghurst's new head gardener Troy

Scott Smith was going through the archives when he stumbled upon an old edition of Hilling's rose catalogue, put together by Graham Stuart Thomas when he was working at the nursery. It was dated autumn 1953 and had been marked up by Sissinghurst's then head gardener, Jack Vass. Jack Vass had noted the roses that had already been planted in Sissinghurst's garden, perhaps as a way of assessing how he could best add to Vita's collection of roses. The tally came to 170. Jack knew there were another twenty-four in the garden that were not marked in the catalogue, bringing the overall number of roses to 194. Curious but not concerned – it was only an observation, after all – he clearly filed the catalogue in his 1953 archives and went out to do his usual gardening chores.

Fast-forward sixty years later. When Troy came across Jack's list in 2013, he paused, and was surprised and shocked. Of the nearly two hundred roses that had been marked in 1953, many were no longer at Sissinghurst. Troy could see that at least a hundred of the roses on Jack's list were missing, and he realised that although Sissinghurst still had approximately two hundred roses, it was clear that at least half of them must have been planted after 1953. The original roses had probably been replaced with other cultivars that were better. It happens in all gardens, particularly National Trust ones. Gardens are works in progress, ever-evolving. However, Troy was still mystified, and he resolved to find the missing roses and replant them in the garden. He resolved to restore Vita's original collection.

In December 2013, Troy ordered many of the replacement roses from Peter Beales as well as other nurseries that specialised in old roses. He also sourced many from overseas. The Peter Beales roses were delivered in February 2014 and planted in time for the flowering season of that year.

Vita's roses were coming home.

Troy's mission to find and replace all of Vita's lost roses is ongoing. He tells me he is still looking for 'lost' cultivars to plant in Vita's rose garden. Some of the roses that have been lost over the years were only 'found' when gardeners discovered old metal labels in a pond. They pulled them out, cleaned them, and added the rose names to the list of varieties to be reinstated at Sissinghurst.

Something else that Troy Scott Smith has achieved during his tenure as head gardener is returning Sissinghurst to its romantic, blowsy, rose-bedecked state. It was no doubt a struggle to persuade the National Trust to allow the garden to become a little more free-spirited, as its creator was. But there is a beautiful balance that is now being achieved between what Sissinghurst was, at the peak of its beauty, and what it has to do now, as a National Trust property. Small steps – but Vita would be pleased.

20

Saving Maud's Roses

'We never truly own gardens, do we? We are simply custodians of them for a while before passing them on to the next generation of maintainers. We are here for a moment in time, yet what we do with that moment rings through decades to come.'

Arabella Bowes, *House & Garden* (2022)

I t is now 2024. Nymans is, like Sissinghurst and Mottisfont and many other great rose gardens in England, in the care of the National Trust. Decades have passed since the great fire and yet Nymans is arguably more beautiful than ever, thanks to both the enchanting ruin of the manor and the beautiful gardens – which continue to be cultivated with the same love that the Messel family showed when they lived here.

Maud's rose garden was redesigned and replanted in the 1980s. It was moved to a new location, to show off her beloved old roses. The new rose garden is an intimate space enclosed by high hedges. At the centre is a beautiful bronze fountain in the shape of a rose.

The space that was the old rose garden, situated to the east of the house, is still there, but it is now a sunken garden with a lawn. It is still as peaceful. Maud replanted this rose garden in 1949-50, with the help of her head gardener James Comber. When Isabella van Groeningen redesigned the rose garden once more, in 1989, and transplanted it to the new location, she found the new space was more accommodating: she could have arches and other structures, and show Maud's roses to greater advantage. In 2006, the decision was made to add to the old roses and extend the planting season by introducing more repeat-flowering roses, or English roses. As a result, Nymans is now full of all kinds of roses, from glorious old varieties to interesting new ones. But the most beautiful roses are still those that clothe the ruin.

What is it about ruins and old roses that appeal to so many of us? Isabel and Julian Bannerman have created successful careers from designing gardens, many of them featuring roses and ruins. The Bannermans' garden projects include wonderful follies and beautiful reclaimed architecture at Highgrove and Woolbeding, among their many designs. Other gardeners are also starting now to buy or lease derelict walled gardens, to restore them and use their sheltered spaces to grow old roses and other flowers.

One of these is Victoria Martin. Victoria is part of a new generation of rose growers who are continuing the tradition of cultivating old heritage roses. Victoria and her husband, Barney, grow mostly old roses in a grand old walled garden in a corner of the Stokesay Court estate in Shropshire. The manor achieved fame after it was featured in the film *Atonement*, but it has always been a remarkable place. The one-acre walled garden, which Victoria leases, is tucked away near the grand stables. It was Barney who found the garden first. And gently pushed Victoria into the idea of growing old roses there, to sell to London florists and other clients.

'My husband Barney and I had been working as Chinese translators, and had been living in Shanghai, where I had designed a few English-inspired gardens,' she explained, in an interview for this biography. 'Tired of the fast pace of Shanghai, we returned to England. Barney was working as a rural surveyor and was at a meeting one day with some land agents when he heard someone say: "Whatever are we going to do about the walled garden at Stokesay." Quickly he said: "Victoria can do that!" But when I came here and stepped through the gate of the walled garden and saw it was an acre I said: "I am so sorry, I think there's been a mistake?"' The size of it was, she said, overwhelming. 'Well, I had to take it, of course. I could not resist the setting, the intriguing outbuildings, and the healthy condition of the garden itself, snug within its high surrounding walls. I think I just I loved the romance of it. I connected with that.' Just as Vita had done at Sissinghurst.

I visited Victoria on a rainy day in June. Shropshire is a three-hour drive from London, so I left early, and as a result I arrived early, and Victoria was with another visitor – a famous garden writer. She asked if I would mind waiting, while she took the famous garden writer to the train station? 'Go inside the garden!' she said. 'Explore it for yourself!' Which is how I found myself walking around this extraordinary walled garden of old roses on a quiet June day, like the character Mary Lennox in Frances Hodgson Burnett's famous novel *The Secret Garden*. I felt as though I had gone back in time to a Victorian garden tended by an army of gardeners. As the garden writer Kendra Wilson wrote in *Gardens Illustrated*: 'Passing through the gatehouse at Stokesay Court in Shropshire, it is possible to believe that you are entering another, better world.'

I spent the next hour on my own, inhaling old roses such as 'Robert le Diable', which is a poem of multi-petalled rosettes with the same rich intense violet-pink colour of my favourite Chanel lipstick. And the once rare 'La Belle Sultane', a deep purple Gallica rose with yellow anthers, a rose of such grace and elegance that it looks like a painting. Victoria agreed with my description: 'It looks like it is glowing,' she said later. When Victoria returned from the station, we walked all the way around the garden in the soft summer rain. And then we retreated to her wonderful potting shed, a grand old brick building with a lovely arched window, where there rested a white jar of gently drooping old roses. Victoria served me a lovely cup of tea with cake, which we ate seated at an old wooden table. There were signs of gardening productivity everywhere: a coat rack groaning with wet-weather coats, a rack of hats, dozens of bunches of dried roses hanging from the rafters. Victoria could see I was entranced by everything, so she said: 'Come and look in here,' and led me to an adjoining room, which was cool and dark. There, down a set of stairs, was the most wondrous sight I had seen in months: buckets and buckets of old roses, waiting to be transported in London. With the filtered light coming in the window, the sight of those roses was magnificent. The scent alone was memorable. If I could have bottled this beautiful cellar of old roses, on this beautiful day, I would.

Victoria grows mostly old roses, among other flowers, which she sells to florists all over England who love these romantic varieties. The well-known florist Shane Connolly described the flowers grown at Stokesay as 'truly among the best in the UK'. 'We grow almost exclusively old roses,' explained Victoria. 'Most are pre-1920, and most of them have evocative French names. But we also have a selection of lovely varieties bred by David Austin, whose nursery is nearby.' Why old roses, I asked? 'They are romantic,' Victoria said simply. 'And they are usually healthy. We love their robustness and generous growth – meaning that we can pick huge boughs of blooms for our clients for them to use in bouquets at parties and weddings. But old roses are also very charming. They really are.'

What was her favourite old rose, I asked her, as we took one last walk around the garden. 'I love 'Charles de Mills',' she confessed. 'But if I could only grow one it would be 'Cécile Brunner'. It lasts for such a long time in a vase.' Victoria then added that she also loved 'Königin von Dänemark', which was first introduced in 1816. She said it was so beautiful, so feminine, that she did a double take when she first saw it.

Later, I read Victoria's blog, in which she had written an article entitled 'Some Roses', perhaps in tribute to Vita's book *Some Flowers*.

'June is the month of roses, in particular old roses, and these are becoming our grand passion', Victoria wrote. 'One great dazzling burst of bloom lasting three or four weeks is the chief gift they give us, but most older roses also have a beautiful softly arching habit, and very interesting leaves, so that they create a lovely appealing backdrop in the garden even when they're not in flower.'

Such was – and is – the success of Victoria and Barney's business, selling old roses to florists from Shropshire to London, that they and their small team soon became overwhelmed with orders. They realised they needed additional growing space. But where would they find another walled garden? One autumn morning Barney took their daughter, Daisy, put her on his shoulders, and went around to all the land agents in the area, asking if they knew of a parcel of land that he and Victoria could lease. The last agent looked at Barney with regret and said: 'I don't know of anywhere, sorry.' But then he paused, and offered a solution. 'I have a walled garden of my own that I am not using. Perhaps you'd like to see that instead?' The land agent's walled garden was two acres – twice the size of Stokesay. But Victoria was prepared. She now manages these two enormous walled gardens of old roses, together with a team of nine part-time gardeners who help cultivate and cut everything. 'It is funny,' she said. 'I hadn't even heard of Shropshire before we came here. But it has such fertile soil. It is been the perfect place to have this business, to learn about these wonderful old roses.'

As I drove back to my hotel, I thought of Victoria, and of Constance Spry and her cutting gardens and passion for old roses, and I marvelled at these intrepid women who take on such incredible projects.

A week later, a parcel arrived at my hotel. It was a gift from Victoria: a book she had written about the best roses for cutting. I was deeply grateful, both for the book and the day at Stokesay. A few months later, I had another email from Victoria. By this time, we had become friends, connected through our love of old roses. Victoria told me that Sissinghurst's head gardener, Troy Scott Smith, had asked her and her team to propagate Vita's 'lost roses', so they could be replanted into Sissinghurst's garden and saved for future generations. Victoria added that she was not the only rosarian entrusted with this task. There were a few gardens that were now growing and saving Vita's roses. But she felt privileged to be one of the few that Troy had asked to protect these precious and rare plants.

I had finished writing the biography by the time this email came, but I inserted this wonderful addendum, this heartening, uplifting postscript. The story, I felt, was now complete.

As I write these final words, on a winter's night in 2024, tucked away in a remote pub in southern England, far from roses, far from spring, I am sanguine. But I cannot help but feel a little melancholy, too. My husband and I have sold our house by the sea, our house with its garden of old roses, our house that has sheltered us through Covid lockdowns, through years of renovations, and the occasional marital disharmony, too. My garden of old roses has been my safe haven for so long that I am not sure how I will survive without it. But I am looking forward to the future, and to spending more time in England, my other home. My other refuge.

The great nature writer Roger Deakin once wrote: 'All of us, I believe, carry about in our heads places and landscapes we shall never forget because we have experienced such intensity of life there ... They live on in us, wherever we may be, however far from them.' This is how I feel about England. It has been my home – and my home-away-from-home – for three decades, since I moved there on a snowy December day in 1994, after a gruelling year of working for the Diplomatic Service during my first year out of university and landed at Gatwick at the quiet hour of 2 a.m. All of London seemed still. As the kind taxi driver drove through the streets to Kensington, it began to snow. I have never forgotten it. I was only supposed to be there a year. I stayed for five. Since then, I have returned, for short and long periods, mostly in the summer when many of the country's gardens become a millefleur of flowers and roses. It is my dream to return here, year after year. Perhaps even to return to live? To walk through the spring woods of Kent and hear the curlews and the willow warblers. To see Sissinghurst Castle again, as the roses bloom. To reconnect with friends – gardeners all of them – and to hear about their garden endeavours, grand and small.

To hear the stories and histories of this gentle land.

And to be enthralled.

Bibliography

Vita Sackville-West

Vita Sackville-West and Harold Nicolson's life at Sissinghurst has been researched, chronicled and written about in dozens of books, biographies, journals and media articles. Vita herself was the author of many books, articles, diaries, letters and notes, some of which are at Sissinghurst and some of which are held in libraries. Most of the writings, stories and events in Vita and Harold's life that are described in this book and in the biographies below are taken from Harold's and Vita's letters, which are now found in the Lilly Library in Indiana, USA, and Balliol College, Oxford. Many collections of her articles for *The Observer* have been in print since the 1950s and are still reprinted in newspapers today. Her columns that became the book *Country Notes in Wartime* are available online, and well worth reading. One of the best collections of her writings is *Vita Sackville-West's Garden Book*, by Philippa Nicolson, published by Michael Joseph in 1968.

Of the many books written about her life and garden, these are some of the most compelling and masterfully written biographies (in reverse chronological order):

Sissinghurst: The Dream Garden, Tim Richardson. Frances Lincoln, 2020.
Behind the Mask: The Life of Vita Sackville-West, Matthew Dennison. William Collins, 2014.
Vita Sackville-West's Sissinghurst: The Creation of a Garden, Sarah Raven. Virago, 2014.
Sissinghurst: An Unfinished History, Adam Nicolson. Harper Collins, 2009.

Portrait of a Marriage, Nigel Nicolson. Weidenfeld & Nicolson, 1998.
Gardening at Sissinghurst, Tony Lord. Frances Lincoln, 1995.
Sissinghurst: Portrait of a Garden, Jane Brown. Harry N Abrams, 1990.
Vita's Other World: A Gardening Biography of Vita Sackville-West, Jane Brown. Viking, 1985.
Vita, Victoria Glendinning. Weidenfeld & Nicolson, 1983.
Sissinghurst: The Making of a Garden, Anne Scott-James. Michael Joseph, 1975.
Diaries and Letters, [of Harold Nicolson], (ed.) Nigel Nicolson. Collins, 1966-68. Nigel Nicolson's edit of Harold Nicolson's. Collins, 1966-8.

Constance Spry

Constance Spry wrote many books during her life. These were all published by J. M. Dent. They include: *Flower Decorations* (1934), *A Garden Notebook* (1940) and ten others. She also wrote many articles for journals and newspapers, including *Country Life, Harper's Bazaar, Journal of the Royal Horticultural Society, The Garden, Tatler* and *Vogue*. Many of her personal papers and records are in the RHS Lindley Library, London. There are many brilliant and fascinating books that also chronicle Constancy Spry's life. Here are two worth reading: *The Surprising Life of Constance Spry*, Sue Shephard, Pan, 2010, and *Constance Spry: A Biography*, Elizabeth Coxhead, W. Luscombe, 1975.

Graham Stuart Thomas

Graham Stuart Thomas wrote many books in his life. These include but are not limited to: *Old Shrub Roses, Climbing Roses Old and New, The Art of Gardening with Roses, The Graham Stuart Thomas Rose Book, The Art of Planting* and *Three Gardens: The Personal Oddysey of a Great Plantsman and Gardener* (memoir), none of which is currently in print.

Charles and Brigid Quest-Ritson are currently finishing a biography of Graham Stuart Thomas's life.

Edward Bunyard

Not a lot has been written about Edward Bunyard, but in 2007 a group of fine writers tried to rectify this with a masterly, beautifully written biography called *The Downright Epicure: Essays on Edward Bunyard,* published by Prospect Books (2007). Other facts and stories about his life can be found in books contained in the RHS Lindley Library in London, where his papers are kept.

Maud Messel

These are two particularly wonderful books that mention Maud Messel: *Nymans: The Story of a Sussex Garden*, Shirley Nicholson, The History Press, 2010, and *Oliver Messel: In the Theatre of Design*, Thomas Messel, Rizzoli, 2011. However, there are many other books about the Messel family, as well as notes and diaries about their lives, garden and achievements at Nymans in England. (National Trust).

Further Reading On Old Roses

RHS *Encyclopaedia of Roses*, Charles and Brigid Quest-Ritson. Dorling Kindersley, 2008.

The Rose, Jennifer Potter. Atlantic Books, 2010.

By Any Other Name: A Cultural History of The Rose, Simon Morley. Oneworld, 2021.

Favourite Roses for Cutting, Victoria Martin. Stokesay Court Walled Garden, 2021.

Rose: A Cultural History of the Flower, Catherine Horwood. Reaktion Books, 2019

Landscape of Dreams, Isabel and Julian Bannerman. Pimpernel Press, 2016.

Chasing the Rose: An Adventure in the Venetian Country. Andrea di Robilant. Allen and Unwin, 2014.

A Green and Pleasant Land: How England's Gardeners Fought the Second World War, Ursula Buchan. Windmill Books, 2014.

The Heritage of the Rose, David Austin, ACC Art Books, 1999.

Orwell's Roses, Rebecca Solnit. Granta Publications, 2021.

Organisations That Promote Old Roses

If you would like to know more about old roses, or perhaps join a society to connect with other rose lovers, there are many organisations that welcome members. In England, there is a wonderful society called the **Historic Roses Group** (**www.historicroses.org**), which seeks to encourage interest in old roses, particularly older roses of historical importance and those no longer widely grown. In the United States there is a similar group called the **Heritage Rose Foundation** (**www. heritagerosefoundation.org**). In Australia, there is a society called **Heritage Roses in Australia** (**www.heritageroses.org.au**), which aims to 'advance the preservation, cultivation, distribution, and study of old garden roses, including roses no longer in general cultivation, roses of historical importance, species roses and their hybrids'. And in France there is a fine organisation called **Roses Anciennes en France** (**www. rosesanciennesenfrance.org/fr**). All welcome new members.

Acknowledgements

This story took me on a grand botanical adventure across England, into walled gardens full of old roses, such as the one at Stokesay Court; into rose gardens I have never visited in all the years I have visited or lived in England, such as Hinton Ampner; into Sissinghurst Castle's garden at dawn, wandering the estate during the bird chorus; into Kiftsgate Court in the Cotswolds on a perfect midsummer's evening after all the visitors had left, when the roses were at their most enchanting; and even into Cecil Beaton's former garden at Reddish House, where roses clothed the house like one of Beaton's finely embroidered gowns. The most memorable part of this grand adventure, the part I am most grateful for, is that it introduced me to some of the most talented (and often most modest) gardeners I have ever met, from famous head gardeners of great estates to the quiet but diligent gardeners who care for the old roses in gardens, grand and small, across England. It is to these people, the unsung heroes of the horticultural world, that this book is dedicated. Storytelling is often about the secrets of people's lives, the untold mysteries and histories. But what it really does is look for and find the extraordinary in the ordinary. And in doing so, it creates a kind of magic. Just as gardens do. I really hope you enjoy this story. And, just as I have had the privilege of doing, I hope you have the chance to visit some of these glorious rose gardens one day, on some splendid summer's afternoon.

I would like to thank the wonderful publishers Gail Lynch and Jo Christian at Pimpernel Press for their kindness and graciousness over the past year, and for publishing this book when many others passed over it. Thanks also to Gemini Books Group, the new owners of Pimpernel, and the brilliant team there including Danny Lyle (who has the patience of a saint!), Mel Sambells, who is the best publicist in the world, and Mylène Mozas, who designed the lovely jacket. I am also grateful to Nancy Marten and David Gaskell for their proofreading and indexing skills.

My heartfelt thanks also go to my editors Charles Quest-Ritson and his wife, Brigid. They are two of the most knowledgeable garden writers in the world, and their thoughtful comments on my manuscript made this book a far better read.

As well, I would like to thank the writer and author Adam Nicolson (Vita Sackville-West's grandson), who was wonderfully hospitable to me at Sissinghurst Castle one summer evening, and Sissinghurst's head gardener Troy Scott Smith, who kindly gave me his time for an interview. I'm thankful to the remarkable garden designers and rosarians, Isabel and Julian Bannerman, who also generously gave their time for an interview. I'm deeply grateful to my friend Victoria Martin of Stokesay Flowers at Stokesay Court in Shropshire for her generosity, friendship and insights into old roses, and to many other new rosarian friends such as Susanne at Dorset Walled Garden and Amanda at Seend Manor Garden in Wiltshire. Thanks also to the staff of the RHS Lindley Library, where I spent many long days doing research, to Hannah at the Alexander McQueen gallery, for one of the most joyful afternoons I've ever had in London, and to Michael Marriott, former head gardener at David Austin and now President of Heritage Roses UK, for his advice on old roses. Something else I will never forget is visiting all the extraordinary National Trust gardens around England and I owe a great debt to the team of the Trust for their kind assistance in researching this book over many years. I would especially like to thank Caroline Ikin at Nymans for providing all the wonderful diary records and notes by and about Maud Messel; John Wood at Hinton Ampner for his charming recollections of working at Mottisfont; Rowena Willard-Wright at Sissinghurst for showing me Vita's personal photo albums and archives, and Jennifer Smith in the National Trust's Image Library who, for many months, kindly helped us select photos and organise licence agreements for both the Trust's images and my own personal photos. The National Trust is an enormous organisation with many moving parts, and I'm constantly astounded at how the team manages everything with grace and patience. It is not an easy job to care for hundreds of England's gardens, especially given the difficulties with ageing estates and the issues of accommodating thousands of visitors through the gates each year. But they do it so that we may enjoy these beautiful places, now and in the future. I am just one of the many grateful souls who returns, again and again, to these beautiful, memorable gardens and houses.

Index

Picture Credits

1 Rosa 'Madame Isaac Pereire', © Janelle McCulloch
2 Sissinghurst Castle, June 1930, © National Trust Images
3 Vita Sackville-West working in the garden, © National Trust Images
4 View of the Rose Garden from the tower at Sissinghurst Castle Garden, Kent, © National Trust Images
5 Vita, Harold and sons at Sissinghurst, © National Trust Images
6 The Rose Garden at Sissinghurst today, Janelle McCulloch, © National Trust Images
7 Sissinghurst garden plan, © Janelle McCulloch
8 Rose Garden in June at Sissinghurst, © National Trust Images
9 Rosa 'Sissinghurst Castle', © National Trust Images
10 Kent landscape, © Janelle McCulloch
11 Aerial view of the Rose Garden, Sissinghurst Castle Garden, Kent Janelle McCulloch, © National Trust Images
12 Sissinghurst Castle Garden, © National Trust Images
13 The Rose Garden in June at Mottisfont, Hampshire, © National Trust Images
14 The Rose Garden in June at Mottisfont, Hampshire, © National Trust Images
15 Old roses in the summer rain © Janelle McCulloch
16 Rosa 'Constance Spry', Mottisfont, © Janelle McCulloch
17 Old roses at Mottisfont, © Janelle McCulloch
18 The ruins at Nymans, West Sussex, © National Trust Images
19 Stokesay Court walled garden, © Janelle McCulloch
20 Roses at Stokesay Court, © Janelle McCulloch
21 A selection of old roses, © Janelle McCulloch